My Three Hats

The autobiography of a schoolgirl at Milham Ford, a member of the Stonesfield Silver Band, and a keen Oxford United supporter

Also by Dorthy Calcutt

The Salt of the Earth (1999)
Born in a Stable (2001)

My Three Hats

The autobiography of a schoolgirl at Milham Ford, a member of the Stonesfield Silver Band, and a keen Oxford United supporter

Dorothy Calcutt

THE WYCHWOOD PRESS

Our books may be ordered from bookshops or (post free) from
The Wychwood Press, Alder House, Market Street, Charlbury, OX7 3PH
01608 811969

e-mail: wychwood@joncarpenter.co.uk

Credit card orders should be phoned or faxed to 01689 870437 or 01608 811969

Please send for our free catalogue

First published in 2003 by
The Wychwood Press
an imprint of Jon Carpenter Publishing
Alder House, Market Street, Charlbury, Oxfordshire OX7 3PH

ISBN 1 902279 15 8

Printed in England by J. W. Arrowsmith Ltd., Bristol

Contents

Acknowledgements

I would like to thank my daughter Madge for relaying this book to a computer disc. Also to Bridget, Richard and Michael who suggested, then goaded then threatened me with a three line whip to get it written.

For photographs, I thank my sister Marion, Terry McCartney, Daniel (my youngest grandson), Godfrey, and Mary Denham. And thank you to Ivor Roberts for the cartoon.

All Oxford United photographs were lent by kind permission of the club. I would like to thank all employees at the club, including Mick Brown, Chris Williams, Tony Bailey, Rosie (Peter Roades-Brown) and Chris Ellis, who have graciously given me their help.

Sorry to all of you who have proved a source of ridicule. I hope I have not lost any friends.

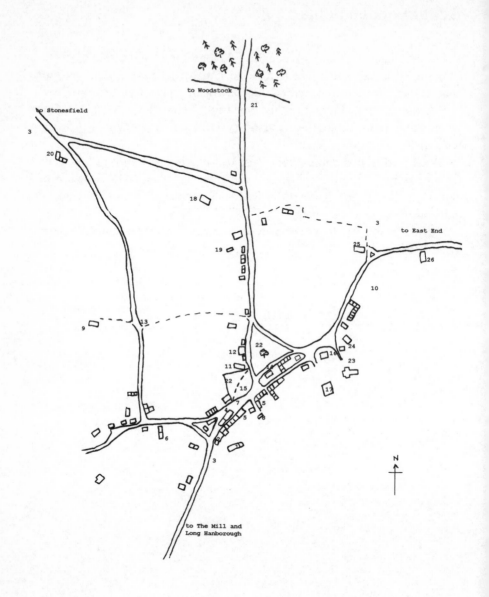

Map of Long Coombe, 1920

Key to map

1	School
2	Marlborough Arms
3	Allotments
4	United Methodist Chapel
5	Shop
6	Gladstone Cottage
7	Outside camp services, later the bus stop
8	The bakery
9	Farm (skimmed milk)
10	Cricket field
11	Coffee house or Tavern
12	Cock Inn
13	Kingdom Pool
14	Royal Oak Inn
15	The old horse trough that I fell off
16	The vicarage
17	Combe House
18	Pig farm
19	Our first home
20	Chatterpie
21	Site of our house – built 1949
22	Village greens, including the oak tree on the main green
23	St Lawrence's church
24	Post office-cum-shop
25	Alma Grove farm
26	Wesleyan Chapel

Florence (3½), Jim (6 months), Dorothy (2)

Preface

I have always thought that my life – starting in a poor but striving family in a rural community in 1920 – has seen more twentieth-century changes than most.

In those days our milk, meat, bread and groceries were all delivered by horse in a variety of vehicles. Combe had no amenities; an urgent message was sent by telegram and delivered by hand. The cricket team still took pigeons to send home their progress. As the crow flies the village was nine miles from the centre of Oxford, nearly six miles from Witney, and two-and-a-half miles from Woodstock (though almost twice that by road!).

All children went to the village school until the age of fourteen. The cane was in frequent use.

The average family had ten or more children, yet they lived in rented or tied two-bedroom cottages.

Girls were forced into private service to give more room both at the table and in bed. Boys were considered an asset. Girls did not anticipate careers, men expected to finance the family and females accepted domination by males.

The village had three fields divided into allotments, and all intensely cultivated. Each grass field contained a pond for the use of grazing animals.

You travelled as far as you could walk. Even the wealthiest farmer went to market in a pony and trap. I remember my brother driving cattle to Banbury market for a neighbouring farmer. That is about twenty miles and he was about fourteen.

Each snippet of medical advice was gleaned from parents or neighbours, as doctors were too expensive.

Everyone attended a place of worship; there were three of them in this village. From a photograph in 1926 there were 35 children attending the United Methodist Chapel Sunday School.

Mothers arose first each morning. After taking up the ashes and cleaning the grate, they lit the fire with sticks to boil the kettle. At the most convenient time there was a dash to the lavatory at the bottom of the garden. It was usually situated next to an occupied pigsty.

The upbringing of children was narrow yet happy and secure; as for the wide, wide world ignorance was considered the best form of protection. Combe had three shops and a Post Office.

Now the village can boast of one or two solitary allotments. I think all the ponds have been filled in. There are no cows, sheep or pigs in the village.

The church still dominates the scenery and one chapel is still in use.

We have one shop and a part-time post office.

My Three Hats

1   Pre-school

I was there all right, but since I remember nothing I relate exactly what my mother told me. On the thirtieth of June 1920, my parents nicely asleep – time about ten o'clock – just about one week early – I decided to say 'Hello' to everybody. It was midsummer when days are longest and weather is expected to be at its best.

This particular night was different; it was very dark and thunder was rolling, rain was clearly imminent. In spite of the weather, Dad got out his bike and hurried off to Combe mill.[1] The local carer – home help, midwife, or whatever name they had then – lived in the cottage that adjoined the sawyer's house. Dad left his bike against the railway fence and hopped over the lines to awake her.

Before she was ready to leave, the heavens opened. The lightning flashed and the thunder came overhead. They were both too scared to face the elements, but a slight lull started them on their journey. Mrs Painting was rather plump, she wore lots of petticoats; I thought she was a comely character but she could not ride a bike. They walked together, all uphill, about three-quarters of a mile to await my birth.

Meanwhile, at Gladstone Cottage, I was impatient and, unaided in a dark room, I entered this world in the middle of a thunderstorm. Mum had no light, the matches were out of her reach, so she could not light a candle. She had no idea of time, so at what time I was born depended on her seeing the clock when the lightning flashed. 'I thought it had just passed midnight so I decided you were born on July the first,' she told me.

I have always been positive in my decisions so I was starting how I meant to continue. My sister had travelled that route only eighteen months earlier, so I must have known the way was clear and it was a one-way street.

My father was Frank Howes, one of five generations who were born and lived their lives in Combe. Combe, originally called Long Coombe, was situated next to the sawmill[1] on the river Evenlode. History dictates that, because of flooding, the monks of Eynsham Monastery carried the church, stone by stone, to the top of the hill and re-erected it on its present site. This happened roughly seven hundred and fifty years ago. Although Coombe means 'a wooded valley' this name continued until 1935 when the railway halt was installed. Whether by accident or design the name 'Combe' appeared on the halt and within a few weeks the road signs were repainted.

It has always been called 'Silly Combe'. The origin of our derisory title is lost in the past. We do have to 'cock a snook' at such statements as 'Putting a pig on the wall to see the band go by'. I wonder why other villages don't have such cultivated pigs?

My father, being a small farmer, naturally craved for a son. I was now his second daughter. What a deplorable night for him, to be woken up, do that journey under extreme conditions, only to find he had a second daughter!

My name had already been chosen, as it had for my older sister, but it still didn't fit. Mother alone made the choice, 'Dorothy', the meaning of which is 'Gift from God'. My parents were very strict 'United Methodists' and by their faith pacifists. During a war they would have been conscientious objectors. Mother's faith was so great that she knew she had been given girls for a specific reason. Maybe one day boys would be conscripted, but girls would not. How right she was!!

I remember little or nothing of my pre-school days. Like all children I was sent out to play when eighteen months old. I had a large scarf around my neck, crossed over and anchored at the back with a large safety pin. There was no danger, I could have fallen in the choicest spot. Yes, there were ditches and puddles, horses and cows passed by, the roads were rough and unforgiving!

When I was eighteen months my older sister – just three – started school. This coincided with the birth of my prayed and craved for brother.

Children's ailments were rampant so the school was closed, but much too late for most families including ours. My sister started the chain, first measles, then chicken pox followed by whooping cough. The doctor was not called but we were carefully nursed back to health while my mother was breast-feeding a newborn baby. 'This is a God sent hardship,' she reflected, 'He will see us through.'

My mother had spent the last four years carrying and nursing babies. How much our lives depended on breast-feeding will never be known but it had given her confidence and strengthened her faith. We had all survived with no side effects, no medicines, no doctor, and no N.H.S. A competent mother must have two qualities. First, to be able to produce a substantial meal with little or no money; second, to understand nursing.

We were very healthy children. An active life both in the garden and road and plenty of sound sleep were the ingredients. We had very few toys; we played mostly in the road avoiding the baker's cart and the horses and cows. Even before I was a year old I was pushed in a pram to the farm about one and a half miles away to enable Mum to plant potatoes. This was considered a female task, and even if she was breast-feeding my brother, she still did it herself.

Why did we only have three children? Perhaps my parents' religion had an influence? The house opposite had ten children. Why? There was another family with ten but their father drank too much.

Another large family lived at Westfield Farm, so they came our way to school. The keeper at Knottoaks[14] had a large family, they too came our way to school. Remembering that children attended Combe School until the age of fourteen, nearly half the pupils came from our direction.

We felt very small and insignificant amongst older pupils.

By January 1923 I was begging to start school, but the schoolmaster insisted that he could not place me on the register. I was however allowed to attend in the afternoons. So it was on Monday July the second that I was put on the register and began what proved to be a lifetime of school attendance.

This gave my mother more time for gloving; making a pair was two hours work but she received one or two coppers – the difference between scraping and planning a meal.

2   Gladstone Cottage

The detached Gladstone Cottage lies at the West End of Combe. My father had bought it for £144 when he returned from Canada; he considered he was now quite wealthy. He had purchased it from the police force – evidently no policeman was needed in Combe anymore! It was a compact, well-built stone cottage in quite a large walled garden. It had Stonesfield slates on the roof, flagged floors, and a lavatory at the end of the garden, but it was strong and outshone many others. It had two quite large bedrooms and the landing was large enough for a single bed. There were plenty of older children to play with but they were members of very large families.

The cottage was very cold; it was heated only by a cooking grate. Most of the heat went up the chimney unless the red embers had been pushed under the oven flue for cooking. A black kettle stood on the hob, always ready for making tea, washing up or even washing oneself. One large, black saucepan stood by it – anything that could help with a stew found its way into that pot. Sometimes it was a rabbit, a pair of pigeons or bones from the butcher. Vegetables in their season, and without exception dumplings, topped it up. Potatoes were placed in a cotton bag and hung from its lid. It was a warming, filling meal and quite truthfully we were well fed. Those dumplings created a comfortable, satisfied inner man, boosting our admiration and appreciation of Mum's cooking. Most food needed in our household was home grown, or legally caught like rabbits, hares or pigeons.

The cottage was, in spite of the fire, very cold. The winters were quite severe. My father would surround all the windows with sticky paper to prevent draughts and ensure that they were never opened. 'If you need fresh air, there is plenty outside,' Dad emphasised. It was so cold, we often woke in the morning to fine the chamber pots frozen.

We had a white-topped table in the centre of the living-cum-kitchen room. Dad had made it prior to getting married. He also bought a Singer sewing machine for Mum as a present. What two valuable items they proved to be: he had his priorities right.

Dad was not alone in small-scale farming; there were about a dozen like-minded males in Combe.

Farming collapsed. The nation was in dept from the First World War. Canada, a country that recruited its workers from England, had introduced combine harvesters. They now exported superior wheat more cheaply than it could be home produced. Farmers now had difficulty in selling any crops, unemployment raised its ugly head. To add to this my father lost several valuable horses. One actually drowned in the river.

Many times Dad contemplated throwing in the towel, as many did. Each year, at Michaelmas, all tenants reported to Blenheim to pay the rent. Several times he went prepared to issue his notice to quit but he was always offered a reduced rent so the hand-to-mouth existence was perpetuated.

Many things needed to be considered. There was very little work available but he had had a variable existence beforehand. Leaving school at eleven he worked in Blenheim gardens, then with the forest hands, then on the estate where his work included building and fencing; thence to Canada, mostly working in concrete. He was well equipped to tackle most local opportunities.

The decision would have been very hurtful. He had designed his whole life making sure that he did not work for others. Most gentleman farmers preferred badly educated labourers who lived in a tied cottage. Dad's situation was very different; we could never be put on the street, as many were. His deep-rooted religion had convinced him that gardening and farming was enjoyable, rewarding, and beneficial, very near to nature and his Maker.

Looking ahead, he had two daughters who, by the age of eight, would be strong enough both to plant and harvest potatoes. This was free labour. My brother would be slowly introduced to the manual work. He could saw wood, light fires and do other innumerable jobs.

We existed.

3   Into the unknown

In January Jim, my brother, was three and like his two sisters before him, he started school.

One Saturday evening my mother had put the galvanised tray in front of the fire for the weekly baths. We followed each other into the bath, Mum boosted the temperature of the bath with a kettle of hot water, always ready. This particular night the kettle was accidentally knocked over just as Jim was stepping in.

The scalds were severe, no skin grafting then. The district nurse, who had just been allocated to Combe and Stonesfield, was called in. Jim did not attend school for several weeks and the schoolmaster was furious. He was proud of his attendance register, and now this three-year-old had given him rows of noughts. The ultimatum came; 'If he does not return soon, his name will be wiped off and he will be excluded until he is five.'

Jim eventually returned and appeased the school master.

By March 1925 the family had settled down again, but one day my Mum had a sudden frightful stomach pain. A cousin had recently died of cancer, so that was uppermost in her mind. A decision was made, a doctor must be called.

He diagnosed appendix trouble and my mother was pleased. She knew that it could be cured, and prayers would produce the desired result. I remember standing behind the ambulance as it drove away. We were told that she would be home in a fortnight. I did not cry, I just stood and prayed as it disappeared from sight. Later we heard the operation was successful, by now the fortnight was nearly through and she would be home...

But one patient had brought in typhoid fever and it galloped through the ward. Visitors were now banned and when or even whether she would come home rested on prayer alone. At home the atmosphere was unbearable. Dad was very worried and stressed. He must continue planting crops. He asked his spinster sister to leave service and look after us. What a shambles! She hadn't a clue concerning children, and indeed my father hadn't either.

I dug in my heels, became very independent, and would not conform; I didn't want help to lace my boots. I must have appeared very ungrateful as indeed I was. She seemed like a usurper and we had no idea if, or whether, it would end. Some well-meaning body had instilled into my father that smoking would ease the tension. I think the culprit was my great uncle John at Freeland.

An ounce of shag tobacco cost seven pence so he bought one ounce and rolled his own cigarettes. Of course it didn't stop there, he was addicted and puffed the filthy fumes around that sealed in room. In fairness, smoking was not considered a health risk. My aunt could not cope with smoke, neither could I, so we coughed endlessly. This proved to be the start of a young life punctuated by coughing. From October till April, with windows taped, I coughed. The outside world thought I had tuberculosis. This continued through my young life until I married and left home.

Mother recovered and came home in June. Happiness at last. Dad hired a local taxi and we all set off to fetch her. This was my first ever car ride and the family was excited. When we reached the railway bridge on the way to Hanborough Dad realised he had forgotten my mother's hat. So necessary was this item that the car turned back to collect it. We didn't object to a longer ride. We brought her home safely, leaving my aunt at home to make a stew. Mother complained about the stew, knowing something was wrong. My aunt had mistaken hyacinth bulbs for onions.

My sister and I had long hair tied with a bow of ribbon and now it was infested with nits. Against all Mum's principles she cut it off. My curls were gone. From now on we had to succumb to the daily ritual. Mother scrutinised our heads. Discipline undermined, my mother resorted to a stick. She placed it behind a picture but I do not remember it ever being used. My mother's devotion to her family had kept her afloat; rigid inflexibility had gone but she would recover it, our beautiful hair had gone, but it would grow again. From now on when not at school we would play in the garden, with the gate firmly closed to avoid re-infection.

Mum always encouraged us to take an interest in the world around us, so although we never ever went to church she did take us down to see the new bells as they stood in the church porch waiting to be hung. Both parents loved the bells and gave a donation to the ringers when they collected on Boxing Day.

We had taken a dislike to breakfast; it was always porridge made with water and plenty of sugar. It was always stodgy so we looked for ways of disposing of it. In all fairness my mother's attempt at porridge was nearly as bad. But Mum was now holding the reins again, she was in charge, and eat that porridge we did – except Jim. We had a passage through to the staircase, the door closed over the first step so there was step projecting that could be sat on. Hence the punishment was to sit there and eat it. Sunday shoes, when polished, were placed on this step until the following Sunday. As my Dad put on his boots one Sunday his feet went into a cushion of stale, stodgy porridge. I think that was the last time Jim was made to eat the stuff. I wonder if he ever eats it now.

Most of our Sundays were spent in chapel and this was no exception. A local prospector had purchased a coach – it held fourteen people and was named 'The Rambler'. A local preacher – Mr John Kibble from Charlbury - had heard of this coach and offered to finance a Sunday school trip taking us to his home in Charlbury. It was the very first coach outing for us so we were very excited.

Mr Kibble had a collection of antiques and many samples of his stone-mason's work. Best of all he had a man trap. I thought this was a good invention. Any intruders deserved such a shock.

The coach was packed to capacity, we were like sardines, and the older members were standing. All went well until, on the way home, we tried to climb the hill between Combe and Stonesfield. We got to the top, then it slithered back to the bottom. Mr Owen Slatter, the coach owner, asked the older boys to dismount and walk the hill while he tried again. A second time when we reached the brow it gave up; so we all had to walk the hill except Mum. In view of her weak state since leaving hospital she was allowed to remain in the coach.

The boys on the coach were fourteen or fifteen years old – already in work – but still wearing short trousers. It was a significant day when they went into 'longs'. It was then a source of ridicule and often induced an inferiority complex.

We headed towards Christmas and everyone who conversed with my parents sympathised with the family.

'Those girls have never had a doll.' I heard the comments.

It was true, but I don't think I ever wanted one. That Christmas our aunts, our friends at the chapel and everyone who knew us well decided to terminate that situation.

We had never seen so many parcels, and, as we unwrapped, we found dolls and more dolls. We had thirteen dolls each and my mother was not amused.

'Why didn't they get clothes, a jumper or socks or even a hat?' She did not see the funny side. I don't think I did either. I had been looking forward to a pair of gloves. I had dropped a hint here and there because my aunt worked at the factory but my hints went unheeded.

4   Combe infant classroom

As I remember it, this room was always overcrowded. There were two steps along one side for the smallest ones to squash on to. There was a black wall for us to write or draw on with chalk. Around the top half of the room were nursery rhymes written in large print with the appropriate pictures. The trainee teacher would point to these words to teach us to read. I already knew all the nursery rhymes from Mum – I would sing them to visitors hoping it would produce a welcome penny. Likewise Mum taught us numbers and how to add them.

There were about one hundred pupils with three teachers. We had neither pencil nor paper. Initially we had a tray on our laps with a handful of sand. We made our names, tapped the edge of the tray, and started again. Most sums were done on the black wall, but sometimes we were given coloured beads, four red, two green, one yellow, five blue and so on. A few large pictures were permanently on the wall. I remember one which read 'I am the Light of the world' and another that said 'Suffer little children to come unto Me'.

It was a Church of England school, so Christianity took the largest share of school hours. We worshipped the same God at the chapel but the teaching was different. At school we learnt the Ten Commandments by heart, in a few years it was the Magnificat, the Nunc Dimittis, the Creed and then on to the Catechism. At chapel we were taught the art of living; the lay preachers would think up their sermons as they cycled along. They belonged to the Oxford circuit so one sermon would be repeated in many villages. The prayers came from the feelings of the preacher, not read from a book.

My parents as Methodists approved of the Ten Commandments as dictated by the Bible but they added many more.

Thou shalt never drink alcohol (except home-made wine).

Thou shalt not swear.

Thou shalt never buy a raffle ticket (gambling).

Thou shalt never play cards.

Thou shalt not, play, buy or sell on a Sunday.

Thou shalt never dance.

Thou shalt not read a newspaper or any secular book on a Sunday.

Thou shalt never go to a horse or dog race.

Thou shalt never wear make-up.

I must admit I did not always understand the commandments from Moses. One said, 'Honour thy father and mother'; one Dad quite near to us was often drunk, causing family rows. What then!?

One said, 'Thou shalt not commit adultery'; I was never offered an explanation as to its meaning.

One said 'Thou shalt not covet'; I was guilty of this one and that very fact worried me. I would love to have played on the village green. The girl down the road had a new bike but she did let me ride it one day. I would have liked a penny to buy my own sweets. (We did get sweets; my aunt would buy a quarter of a pound for two pence in the market. Mum kept them in a tin and allocated us one each at bedtime.)

Those early years were rigid and severe but always consistent and secure – it would be called monotonous today but we did not see it that way. Mum spent many hours making our clothes from cast-offs brought home by her sisters in service. That sewing machine was very overworked.

5   Medicine or lack of it

Our local doctor lived in Woodstock; he drove to Combe on a motorbike. He had to be paid so he was seldom called, but if the situation warranted it, he would dispense the medicine in the surgery. No tablets then, it was always in a bottle and tasted horrible.

The Radcliffe Infirmary was financed very differently. Each adult in Oxford and the surrounding villages paid two pence a week as an insurance against being admitted if needed. My father was one of the village collectors in Combe. This fee also included all children under fourteen. The fee for fourteen and fifteen year olds was one penny each week. In addition, during Easter week we canvassed from door to door collecting eggs. This ensured each patient a boiled egg for Easter Sunday breakfast. Hens were then bred and fed naturally, so like all birds they only laid eggs in the spring and summer. There was a glut at Easter and none at Christmas. Most competent housewives stored eggs in isinglass to use in the winter. Most villagers kept hens and would expect our annual call. My father's situation was different, as he was self-employed, he paid into an insurance scheme. It was called The Oddfellows, and I believe it still exists.

This is a moot point – why did he always have the flu every winter? The doctor was called and he received two weeks' benefit. I have known him get up early – cycle to the farm to feed the horses and any other livestock – then back home to bed with a cup of hot Bovril to await the doctor. I have actually been at home with my severe smoking cough – shut in my bedroom with the bedclothes over my face and a large handkerchief to stuff over my mouth – and told to keep quiet while the doctor visited. If he had heard me it would have meant that awful medicine plus a dreaded doctor's bill.

My mother kept a few first aid items. Always a jar of Vaseline, a bottle of camphorated oil, and a lump of Snowfire for Dad's hands, because they chapped easily when ploughing in the winter. There was a bottle of Lysol – in a very dark bottle with pimples – for a disinfectant, which was dabbed on grazed knees or elbows or even boils or sores. As she was loath to throw anything away, old clothes were torn into strips for bandages.

Mum used a few homemade remedies, the best being blackberry vinegar. There was an unlimited supply of the fruit so the drink was made very strong and was diluted with very hot water. It was a natural fruity drink, very warming indeed. My Dad would drink her hot elderberry wine.

The one thing I hated was onion gruel. I loved raw onions, fried onions, boiled in stews but not, not, gruel. It looked like weak cornflour with lots of onions but they pretended it would cure my cough, so because I refused to eat it they tried to drench me – just like Dad drenched his animals.

I was wrapped in pink thermogene,[10] both chest and back, for weeks. It smelt of iodine and in theory it should have stopped my cough. It didn't. Why, why did I have to suffer just because Dad insisted with his smoking?

Mum also made ginger tea. She smashed root ginger with a hammer, then steeped it in boiling water – it did not stop the coughing but it was pleasant to drink and would relieve the pain of indigestion. Dad sometimes had a mustard bath. He immersed his feet in a bowl of hot water with mustard. I've no idea how or why that made him feel better.

6   A day in the life of a four-year-old

I was wakened just before eight each morning. My mother was always there to help, but mostly we put on the exact clothes we had taken off the previous night. In the winter our vests were already on. We added our 'combs' (combinations), under bodice, petticoats, jumpers and skirts. We had woollen, well-darned, hand-knitted socks and equally well-soled lace-up boots.

Under supervision we knelt by our beds to say our prayers. That is exactly what we did, we did not pray, it was just 'God bless mummy, God bless daddy'. Our parents determined that this would help our pattern for life.

Down to breakfast and, 'For what we are about to receive, the Lord make us truly thankful'. I doubt if we were ever thankful for stodgy porridge and cocoa made with water. Then, a 'thank-you' grace for something we hated.

Farming was at a very low ebb, so at this time Dad had very little stock on the farm. He did not keep milking cows so one of us was sent to the local dairy farm with an enamel, pint-sized milk can to collect a pint of skimmed milk. It was a white can with a blue rim. I thought I was very clever because I could swing it round in circles, never spilling a drop. I had never heard of centrifugal force but I was already learning about it.

School, only a few yards away, opened at nine. After prayers and register, it was always scripture, sums and writing, in that order – then home to dinner at midday. Grace again, both before and after the meal. I do not remember a lot about those meals, but they did appear to be dominated by 'bubble and squeak'. We often had an apple pudding boiled in a basin with a cloth over the top. This were delicious; the apple was pink because it was overcooked, but nevertheless it looked and tasted superb.

We arrived back at school at half past one. Stories, drawings, and poems seemed to fill most of the afternoons till we went home again at half past three.

Dad's dinner was usually warmed for him, while we had bread and jam, butter or dripping. During the winter months we would take turns sitting on the peg rug[15] by the fire making our own toast. We liked that; it was very tasty with beef dripping. We finished our tea with a slice of cake, usually dough cake.

After grace, we – the females – all helped with the washing up. This was done in an enamel bowl with a knob of soda added to the water. We had no mains water or any amenities. Our water was pumped from our individual pump in the lean-to washhouse, and very good clear, sparkling water it was, coming from the underground spring. When it was dark, we had a paraffin lamp on the table and Mum would sit close to it, still stitching gloves.

Sometimes Dad would have a choir practice. Combe had a good village choir and the bass section would strive to produce perfection. There were Jess Moss and Mr Bevan, the head teacher, and Dad. They used our small harmonium in an effort at tuning. I remember one year when 'The Hallelujah Chorus' was the choice for a contest in Witney. 'All hail the power of Jesus' Name' seemed to be their warming up piece. Most nights he would put his feet on the mantlepiece, and read the newspaper and impose several items from it on us. Political news always took priority, he was a Liberal supporter. Mum always told me he did this to enhance his reading ability as he had left school at eleven.

Mother supervised our washing; first the face, round the ears, then the hands and last a determined effort on the knees. After a trip to the lavatory with a candle, mother escorted us up the stairs. There was one stone hot water bottle in the family but Dad used that. We had pint-sized earthenware fizzy pop bottles. They did not stay hot for very long but sleeping was never a problem.

After listening to our prayers, Mum tucked us in, making sure we were warm enough, gave us one boiled sweet, kissed us and left the room leaving the door open. We were all three sleeping in the same room at that time; I was a very sound sleeper.

7   1927

It was in the early spring that one Tuesday I went into the village with Rose Betts. We knew her extremely well; she spent many hours with us as her gran was our neighbour.

Mum approved of Rose and Rose approved of Mum's apple pudding. It was a standing joke that she could smell it from her own bed. Mum always used cloves, unlike Rose's mother, hence the attraction. Even so my mother was loathe to allow us to play on the village green, as she preferred us to be where she could keep on gloving but simultaneously keep one eye on us. In spite of this we were playing around the old horse trough – pushing each other. I was the one that fell off. My arm was hurting so miserably I walked home alone. I complained but Mum had no mercy. 'If you disobey, it's your fault.'

This happened on Tuesday and for the next few days there were screams when I was dressed or undressed but never, never one bit of sympathy.

As we were walking to the farm on Friday we met the district nurse. Mother stopped her and asked her to look at my arm. 'You must take her to the doctor' she advised, 'I think there is a fracture.' This would mean a walk through Blenheim Park, which was quite usual. This time Mum refused to take me, as there would be a bill to pay and Mum did not write cheques. So as Sunday morning was Dad's first available time, that was settled.

I remember that walk very well. Dad knew the park and every tree in it. He had lived near its wall as a boy, then on leaving school he had worked first at the palace, then in the gardens. He worked with the foresters helping to plant the elm trees on monument plain. The whole estate was nostalgia to him.

I lapped it up; I learnt about trees, birds, fish and flowers. This was my first yet most memorable combined nature and history lesson I ever had. We saw several red squirrels.

We went to Dr Mogg – he lived on the bank. He diagnosed a slight fracture of the collar bone. He strapped it down to my side – leaving an empty sleeve. Keep it there for a month, then it can go into a sling. A nice big cheque for seven shillings and sixpence was paid, and I was not allowed to forget it.

I could not now use the toilet unaided so I had to stay away from school.

Mum had seen an advertisement for a sock-making machine together with enough wool to make dozens of pairs of socks. There was a lull in the glove making industry, so she launched into a new venture. Although this skill was unknown to her, she concentrated until she was churning out men's socks in the hundreds. They emerged from the machine in one long strip, filling the clothes-basket placed underneath. Dad would cycle to Hanborough station collecting bales of wool and returning the socks. Mum was becoming the breadwinner; she still prick-seamed any gloves she could get and she still did the white washing for a few neighbours.

Easter in that year saw the biggest change ever in the educational system. All pupils between the ages of eleven and fourteen would be bussed to Church Hanborough – and secondary schools were born.

Both the headmaster and assistant left Combe School and Miss Ruth Walker was appointed as head. At the same time all eleven-year-olds were to take an exam and the so called winners – about one per cent – would qualify for grammar school education. The examination was in two parts, and although Combe had no *winners* during the first three years I do remember Gilbert Betts and Gwen Johnson (now Bishop) getting past the first hurdle.

Combe was in a very unlucky situation. We were a county school where no county grammar school existed. There was a halo of small schools around the city all in this unfortunate position.

This simplification of school standards created untold family and village troubles. While Gilbert was receiving praise, his brother Reg was kicking over the traces and behaving appallingly both in and out of school. He and his friends were caned daily at school; the schoolmistress was loosing control.

When you run a race, no matter how many runners, there is only one winner; the others are losers – this we all clearly understood.

Is education a race? It was then that the rat race for education began.

8   Sunday in 1929

Whatever we could *not* do on Sunday, we were allowed to eat.

My mother was first downstairs, lighting the fire, taking up ashes etc. She made a suet crust, placed the meat inside, often a rabbit but if not it was a pound of shin of beef at a cost of sixpence. This was boiling on the hob before anyone else was down. It was left there, untouched until noon and was usually very well cooked. Occasionally it went off the boil so it was tough, and once the saucepan had tilted into the fire – some mess!

The potatoes were placed in cold water and left on the hob, praying they would be boiled and cooked when we arrived home. The greens, usually cabbage were cooked afterwards. I remember little about our 'afters', jam tart with custard sometimes.

We, the children went to Sunday school at ten o'clock, getting home again in time to use the lavatory and be back for service at eleven.

I remember so many of those preachers. John Kibble the stonemason from Charlbury, Will Watts of Elsfield (he was an uncle of the Collier family), and

John Brownjohn who lived in Plantation Road and was a college guide. Mr Brownjohn escorted the Sunday school around the colleges once at top speed. I well remember the sweet shop at the end; he bought us some sugar candy. It was made from a super-saturated sugar solution. A string was left in the solution and crystals formed around it. Thank you Mr Brownjohn, it was unforgettable.

There was also Mr Martyr, the gent's hairdresser, Mr Broadribb, the cycle shop owner, Mr Frank Fox, the owner of Kemp Hall Press, and Mr Colegrove, who owned the educational supplier in Queen Street.

They had various ways of getting to Combe; some were brought by car, some could even drive, and Mr Watts always cycled, but John Brownjohn in tailed suit always walked. He was so eccentric, walking so fast, he would walk the countryside, round North Leigh and Stonesfield and returning to evening service at five-thirty. He often didn't make it, arriving late – but he insisted this walking gave him inspiration. After morning service the preacher would have midday meal with Mr and Mrs Busby who lived in 'Evenlode'.

We children were due back at chapel at two o'clock. My father was super-intendent so he took the afternoon Sunday school. We sang the usual hymns, 'Jesus Loves Me', 'Jesus Bids us Shine' and 'What a Friend we have in Jesus'. Although Miss Putt from the post office usually played the harmonium, it was beginning to get difficult to find a pianist. So the money was somehow going to be found to teach my older sister to play the piano. She went each week to Mr W.Oliver, the church organist. 'Thou shalt not covet' loomed up in me as jealousy raised its ugly head.

After Sunday school we went back home for tea and often took the chapel preacher with us. If we had such a visitor we always went into the front room, using Mum's best crocheted tablecloth and the best tea set from the glass cabinet. Of course best table manners had to be switched on and that included very little talking.

Next service started at half past five so – no time to lose – it was back to chapel. This service lasted a bit longer, but there was plenty of singing. By now I had learnt most hymns by heart, but I didn't always understand them. The list included 'Jesu, Lover of my soul', 'Rock of Ages Cleft for Me', and 'Onward Christian Soldiers'. Why didn't they have words that I could understand? My favourite was, 'If You have a Kindness Shown; Pass it on'. After the service, still kneeling, we sang one more. It was either, 'Abide with Me', or 'The day Thou gavest, Lord is ended'.

After this, in summer we went for a family walk, but in winter one or two relatives would be invited home for a cup of tea. Out came Dad's gramophone; it had a handle to wind it and a rather large horn. This gramophone had recently pushed out Dad's melodeon. What was played on that gramophone? You've guessed it – hymns. Many were the identical hymns we had been singing all day. Still we loved it. Most families did not have such a luxury.

There was one record that had been criss-crossed with a red-hot poker. It must have been too bad for our ears.

In the United Methodist circuit we had a Monday night get-together. The Olivet at Woodstock, or the Bladon branch, or ours at Combe, took turns in being host. There were readings, solos, and hymns and refreshments afterwards. It was called Christian Endeavour and we relished it.

Worship over, we now had six days to live in the style of all we had learnt.

9   Pastimes in the twenties

We did not see our childhood as humdrum. We could always find a piece of limestone and draw a hopscotch base, 'fag cards' were plentiful, and boys spent hours 'flicking' them, both winning and losing. Marbles were a valuable property. We would walk down to Kingdom Pool collecting rushes to plait. We would hunt for efts; they are the offspring of newts. Among the possessions we could rely on was a piece of string to use for skipping, some marbles, a hoop, and a ball. We would throw the ball against a wall and catch it on the rebound.

Whips and tops could be used in the road but were banned in the playground. The singing of 'The farmer's in his Den', or 'In and out the Windows', or even 'Alley, Alley, O' or 'Oranges and Lemons' echoed around during school break. We used gloving thread to spin buttons, and thin string to make a 'cat's cradle'. During Friday afternoons we were allowed in the school field which we shared with cattle. Controlled games were rounders or stool ball. On hot Wednesday afternoons the teacher would take us to the river for swimming lessons. We also shared that with a herd of cattle.

We were content with our lot; either designing our own games or trying out those handed on by word of mouth.

After a fall of snow we would walk to the farm where there was a steep grassy bank. We loved to toboggan, occasionally coming to a sudden halt in the hedge or wall at the bottom.

We always anticipated with pleasure our Easter chapel anniversaries, which included a visit, on Monday, of friends from the Rose Hill chapel in Oxford. They in turn gave us a social of hymn singing.

The first Sunday after the tenth of August brought Combe Feast. Horse-drawn vehicles moved in bringing their stalls and wares. Galloping horses, swings and donkeys filled the green. Rifle ranges, coconut shies, sweet stalls and 'penny-a-pull' took up their prearranged sites. There was a huge hammer where the strongest tried to ring a bell.

This was the village event of the year and I had a penny to spend. I always chose a ride on the swings in the afternoon because the ride was much longer in daylight hours. Acetylene lamps buzzed all around as night crept in unnoticed. Squibs[11] were chasing the girls as we chewed our brandy snap. Too much beer was being drunk at The Cock and The Royal Oak but we were ushered well away. This was the first time I ever saw fish and chips being sold from a mobile van.

In September we spent many hours picking blackberries. Mum made lots of jam and blackberry vinegar. We were taught the reasoning behind preparing for winter.

At this time the teacher started a Girls' Friendly Society. We used the room over the games room at the tavern. Oh dear! Oh dear! She agreed with playing cards. It was there, unknown to my parents, I learnt to play 'snap' and 'strip jack'.

During these years Combe had developed an extremely good cricket team and the football team wasn't bad either. I took an interest in both teams and soon understood the finer points. Once we were taken in a coach to a cricket final in Witney. The coach echoed with, 'We've won the cup', and 'Show me the way to go home', on returning.

On Saturday mornings we always waited for the butcher's horse and cart. We knew her well as Mrs Tidmarsh gave us a lump of suet. She took her five-year-old daughter into our house and breast-fed her. I was not surprised, I just thought it was weird. Was there some satisfaction for mother or child or was it an insurance against another birth? I personally thought we were grown up and she was not.

So much of our family time was spent walking to and from the farm. I remember in the late twenties being sent from the farm to my uncle's house. He had a cat's whisker wireless set, which gave out the weather forecast. A farmer really needed to know if a corn rick[12] should be covered with a tarpaulin or not.

10   Combe School 1930

The carrot that had been dangled before us was still dangling. No scholarship had been won, and my sister was now in the top class with many more. Probably seven or eight; that was a large class for Combe School. There were only three scholars in my year; unlike me, the other two had started school very late so we were a very difficult class to teach. I was therefore pushed on a year and the other two held back a year. The teacher did have four school years to teach.

I was good at sums. It does help when you are encouraged and told what a difference education makes to your life. My mother used to say, 'Any possession can be stolen, but not education, it can never be taken from you. Don't bother about history, that's gone, and don't worry about drawing. Concentrate on sums and writing,' she urged. We were trained in pounds, shillings and pence, hundredweights, pounds and ounces, gallons, quarts and pints, fractions and decimals.

The county had an ultimatum – they must award scholarships even if they had no grammar school. The winners (I did hate that word) must go to school in the city. This was severe on the county, who would have to provide tuition fees, books and transport to and from school.

This particular year three grammar school places were granted; one to a girl from Littlemore, one from Wolvercote and one to my sister from Combe.

Now the question arose, could my parents afford it, could my sister physically undertake the journey? We lived three miles from Hanborough railway station. The walk from Oxford station to the school on The Plain was nearly as long. My sister would leave home about seven-thirty and arrive back at six-thirty. Often it would be barely daylight when she left home and very dark before she left school to start the long journey home. That return journey in winter was daunting even if the weather was favourable. The only bicycle light was an oil lamp, which blew out with the least puff of wind. On the benefit side, tuition was free, books were provided, as were a new bike, a season ticket for the railway journey and a uniform grant.

Mother insisted she would do the best she could for her offspring.

Dad pretended he had no say, but he easily agreed. The grammar school had long holidays compared with the local school. There would be four weeks holiday at Easter, coinciding with potato planting. Seven weeks in August and September that happened to be harvest time for both corn and potatoes. Who would be the winner? My sister would have a good education and at the same time my Dad would get free labour. I do not mean to be unkind to my father, as he had gone through ten years of poverty. Unemployment was rampant, the general strike did not help, the Wall Street crash shook the world, then came the Jarrow March.

'The darkest hour of the night is the hour before dawn'. How true this proved to be! The Women's Institute had started in Combe in 1931; my mother was a founder member. She at least would have one hour a month away from the family. Dad, for the first time, was left with his family. Employment in the area was improving, thanks to William Morris. Men, even from the small villages, were beginning to leave the farms and filter through to the Cowley works. William Morris was being proclaimed a distinguished pioneer with foresight; he was heading the vanguard of easier travel.

1930 was also the year when a sugar beet factory was opened at Eynsham. A new crop was introduced to farmers. This would mean even more work, but alas women and children could do much of it.

Several of the local preachers discussed the possibility of Dad growing vegetables and sending them to their houses by carrier. This would be of mutual benefit to seller and buyer. What a chance to help villagers! The Women's

Combe School, 1929. Nine of the girls were called Dorothy.

Institute picked up on this, and started their venture, opening up a stall in the open market in Oxpens in Oxford. This was the scene of the cattle market and fresh produce was tempting.

Dad concentrated on a few acres near the farm barn, every imaginable vegetable was grown, extra hens were kept, and sales multiplied.

My mother had cash in hand each week – she had never had it so good. She continued to be very economical, saving enough to purchase a greenhouse for tomatoes, pot plants and bedding plants. The venture was rolling. The number of greenhouses increased, the garden was a hive of activity. Customers came in from the village and further away. It was proving difficult to keep up with supplies, yet this was at a time when all allotments were being cultivated.

11   Work! Work! Work!

My sister had started her grammar school education in September 1930. She found it physically very difficult, but she kept going and truthfully she got no sympathy at home. I was warned it was my turn next year.

My mother worked every minute, according to the length of daylight hours or suitable weather. The number of gloves coming from the factories was now declining. Sometimes there was an ample supply of wool for socks, but not always.

I had been left alone in the top class of Combe School. The school now had only twenty-six pupils as the seniors had now left. My family, which had appeared so small when we started, now qualified as one of the biggest. Several children now belonged to families of one or two.

I was often left unattended to do my sums. I loved it, in fact the teacher bought a book of algebra for me to work out equations. I was often given errands to run. On Monday mornings some children took pennies to school to buy stamps. When twelve stamps had been stuck on a card, the resulting shilling was banked. I was the one who went to the post office each week.

At this time the school had a mobile dentist; poor children had not received dental treatment before. I remember that dentist very well; he had auburn, curly hair and spoke with a Scottish accent. Facilities were non-existent, we were ushered to the pump in the schoolyard to wash out our mouths. There was just one enamel cup hanging on the pump and we all used it. I don't think we ever thought it was unhygienic.

This particular year there was a keeper's family living at 'The Weir'. They had failed to return the signed form for the treatment. I was sent to their home to collect it. When I approached the five-barred gate at the high bridge there was a herd of cows on the other side. I was supposed to be used to cows and therefore not expected to be afraid; but I really was scared. I stood there for a few minutes: should I go back to school to be ridiculed or should I brave it out? Ultimately I put my hands together and prayed as never before, then smartly opened the gate and walked deliberately amongst the herd. They followed me to the house and back again. 'Aren't you afraid of them?' the mother asked me. I answered with an emphatic 'No.' I only hope that white lie was cancelled out by my faith in prayer.

I remember coughing incessantly that day, so I was sent to shop for medicine and was given it at school with no effect.

The forthcoming examination depended on both arithmetic and writing; my writing and spelling was not good. This year, also, there would be only one place granted in the area that surrounded the city. Chipping Norton school was already in the pipeline.

I knew I could do the sums, but the essay ('composition' we called it) would be my Waterloo. There was a choice of two; the first suggested title was 'Presence of mind'. The second was the first sentence of a story and we had to imagine the rest.

The story was, 'One day I was walking in the woods and came to a cross-roads'... This was made for me, but I often wonder if any pupil chose the first. What could an eleven-year-old write on that subject? Did any pupil really understand it?

Work for the night is coming, work thro' the morning hours.
Work while the dew is sparkling, work 'mid springing flowers.

Work when the day grows brighter, work in the glowing sun.
Work for the night is coming, when man's work is done.

This was one of the hymns we continually sang.

The examination now behind me, my energy was channelled into weeding vegetables. Rows and rows of onions, carrots, beetroot, spinach, and lettuces. A job destined for women or children, and I was the only one now with time after school.

Our house on Saturday mornings was like a shop – anything would sell, with so many outlets, including the carrier, the W.I. market, and the locals. It was difficult to keep up with supplies. Crops that Dad had never before grown were embarked upon; endive, New Zealand spinach, mushrooms, forced rhubarb, and pot plants including cinerarias and gloxinias. Everything that could be grown in England, Dad grew. He even introduced Welsumer hens because their eggs had very brown shells and that pleased the customers.

Mum was aggrieved that my sister could now bike to the farm but she still had to walk. She had no bike, she had not even tried to ride one. What a blessing if she could! She bought one and Dad tried to teach her. It was a long, painful process, but after many arguments, several falls and sprained ankles she overcame the handicap. That spring was spent in weeding, selling and delivering.

May brought the confirmation of my scholarship. I would emulate my sister. I remember the interview I had with the head teacher. 'You are not just going to school any more,' she said. 'You are coming here to be educated for a career.'

That was news to me, it puzzled me; until now I had thought of my future being with someone who had Christian principles; who, like me, wanted a happy, lively, family. I admired my mother and had already decided to adhere to her ideals and judgements.

12   My first day at grammar school

One Friday in September 1931 I started my expected education at Milham Ford School.

Rising about six-thirty, first breakfast, which was now bread and milk which I preferred to porridge. There was now full cream milk delivered by two farmers' daughters from Alma Grove farm using a pony and float.

I had very long coarse hair, so after a face wash I plaited it. It was up to me to prepare a midday lunch but there was very little choice. Mum held on to her beliefs and always bragged that she never bought food in a tin. The only exception was golden syrup. Hence there was nothing except homemade jam to fill a sandwich. I sat by the fire and made myself two pieces of toast – who cares if it is cold by midday? The real trouble was that Mum (or should I say Dad?) preferred cottage loaves so the shape of my toast looked ridiculous. I spread dripping if it was available – and it usually was because the butcher gave away lumps of beef fat.

Then at 7.30, wearing my newly bought uniform, riding my recently acquired bike and with my satchel over my shoulder, I donned my school hat and gloves and was off.

There was a long downhill ride to the river and railway line, then an uphill struggle into Hanborough. This steep hill just had to be walked. After that another long hill down to Long Hanborough railway station. We completed those three miles by about eight o'clock. Our bikes now left in the goods shed, we caught the 8.10 stopping train to Oxford. (After leaving Oxford it was an express train to Paddington so many passengers were en-route to London. I'd never heard of commuters then.) So with a wave of a green flag and a guard's whistle, the signal turned to green, the engine blew its whistle and blasted out its excess steam, then chugged its way to Oxford. There were already about six similarly attired girls in one carriage so we always travelled together. The train ride was usually uneventful so we arrived at Oxford station at 8.35.

We left the bustling, crowded platform and the smell of steaming trains, went down into the subway and out into Oxford. In those days trains were still steaming in and out of the L.M.S. station, their smells overwhelmed by Frank Cooper's marmalade factory exactly opposite. We made our way up Park End Street and over the bridge by the icehouse. A row of very small cottages clung to the canal. This was Fisher's Row and suddenly I realised that all city inhabitants were not rich, and our own cottage was far superior to these.

Leaving behind the smell of the marmalade another smell – unknown to me – was entering our nostrils. It was the brewery – the word beer was taboo in out household so the smell had no effect on me whatsoever. The words 'beer' and 'brewery' I did not even link together. I did know that if Dad's barley harvest was good it was sold for malting.

We approached Carfax where one policeman wearing white gloves took centre stage. The smell of the freshly ground coffee from the Cadena café took over. We never ever drank coffee at home but I loved that smell. Down High Street we went, along pavements where gratings covered large kitchens below. This was the time of day when the smell of bacon was wafting in the breeze.

By now my leg muscles were telling me they did not like pavement walking but on we went over Magdalen Bridge, where floods of cyclists were pouring into the city, past the college and down 'The High'. Since we arrived about five minutes passed nine, and assembly was at 8.50, we were excused assembly and went straight to our classroom.

The first day at school was taken up by an introduction to our form mistress. She dictated the school rules. Then we had sheets of foolscap paper to write down every book we would need for a year's work. Poor me! I had to write it twice, one went to Blackwells and one to Oxfordshire Education Committee. This was an enormous task. Oh, how I wished we could do some sums. Our form mistress happened to be one of the school maths teachers, and I knew I would find favour with her.

Timetables had to be written. There were subjects I'd never heard of, there were French and Latin. Why did we have to learn Latin, if my whole life was going to be spent raising a healthy, happy family? Dozens of workbooks were handed out and they all had to be taken home to have margins drawn on every page. I wondered what would go into those margins in weeks ahead. My satchel was going to prove very heavy travelling home that evening.

School hours were completed at four but we were not allowed to leave until 4.35, giving just time enough to catch the 5.30 stopping train home. On the return journey Jimmy Dingle was methodically pacing up and down Cornmarket as a sandwich man while shouts of 'All the latest news' and 'Read all about it' were heard from the base of Carfax tower. Our small train was linked with the London train due at five twenty five.

Our bike ride home was much more strenuous, so much uphill and now I was weighed down by books. I arrived home exhausted and knackered. I collapsed into a chair and admitted I would never be able to continue.

Those daily journeys resembled a modern day triathlon.

13   Language is difficult

My first suggested essay appeared simple.

I had to pretend that a visitor was travelling by coach to my home. I just had to write a detailed description of the route from the coach stop to my home.

At this time the coach stopped in the open space in front of our chapel. This was a very short walk so I had to waffle a bit. We had no road names or house numbers in the village so what could I say? I just said, stand with your back to the church and proceed forward: this will be due west. There will be puddles on the road – there always were – the road would be rough. You may see girls skipping or boys playing marbles – if you are not sure you can always ask them. Our cottage is called Gladstone Cottage, it is the second on the left.

When this effort came back to me there was a dreaded red pen put through it and in the margin written alongside was the word 'RETURNED' in red capital letters. There were a few rows of writing in red pen that firmly emphasized, 'You have not given the name of your street. You have not given your house number.' I found one other girl who was treated identically. The teacher stormed at us in class making us feel both stupid and inferior.

After the lesson I somehow plucked up the courage, went up front to speak to her explaining the situation. Who was looking stupid now? She tore out the first page of my book which meant my book now started at page two. We had previously numbered the pages so this could never happen. I received no apology, but the damage was done. This episode had done nothing for the persecution and tactical bullying I received about my background.

My needlework in the first term fared no better. The teacher was French but she doubled as needlework teacher. She was a fussy, bustling, frenzied, frantic type, always over-enthusiastic and animated. In no uncertain terms she told us we were never to be seen sewing without our thimbles. The first term we were going to do 'drawn thread' work. I understood this as my mother had already taught me. Worse was to follow. 'Please bring a piece of 'huckabuck tarlin' next week,' she demanded. I didn't understand what she said or meant and she was quite unapproachable, so I decided not to explain to Mum that week.

The following week I listened carefully as she repeated the same words. I did see the material that others had brought but I had never seen such material before. This continued through the term and I never did produce the necessary material. I did know that her French-Oxford accent was cultivated and far removed from my natural Oxfordshire accent. She always understood me but not *vice versa*. As she repeated the word 'tarlin' she was manipulating her tongue around her mouth and out came the word of two syllables when I thought it should have been three. She was in fact saying 'towelling'. My mother would have understood, as when in service she had made guest towels of the same material, but even in 1931 it was considered old-fashioned.

In any case Mum could not have gone to the shop to purchase it, as the draper only called once a month, so we would order one month and receive delivery the next.

14   Facing realities

My accent was ridiculed, openly by the girls, more discreetly by members of staff. A few of the wealthier girls had elocution lessons so it was suggested that such lessons would help me. I was still living in the same household, hearing the same accent as before and no way could my parents either afford or permit such lessons. They were humiliating and in my family would be treated as snobbery.

I did go to one lesson; I was no hope. I knew I would excel at physical exercises and games. Some girls had too many airs and graces to even want to run a race, do a cartwheel or play a game of hockey. Although the class was divided as for our likes and dislikes, we were all obliged to partake in sports. We did our sports in gym knickers and blouses and my parents were horrified.

Winter months introduced us to both hockey and netball and I excelled in both. Summer was cricket and tennis, the latter being too expensive for me; I avoided it, concentrating on cricket. Everyone, including the games mistress, marvelled at my knowledge of cricket, but in all fairness they had not been reared in the village of Combe.

Most girls were only interested in tennis. It was considered to be more genteel. 'Cricket!' they said, 'That's a boy's game!'

The games mistress also did remedial lessons with girls who had flat feet or any other disability. It was expected that I would suffer from rickets or something caused by lack of a balanced diet. My feet passed inspection; indeed they have never given me a problem. They had walked so many miles in my short life. My legs proved to be straight and after much rubbing, my spine was also passed fit. 'You do have one shoulder lower than the other,' she noticed. So she asked me to attend remedial classes as soon as I arrived at school. 'I'm very concerned with this red mark on your shoulder.' I picked up my laden satchel to return to my classroom; then casually I commented, 'There's too many heavy books to carry.' She did not call me back for any future classes.

It wasn't only my accent but my vocabulary that was so narrow and stifled. Topics in our family were politics, the chapel, and crops and animals on the farm. None of these topics were understood by my classmates. Girls living in the city had a broader outlook, they had money to spend. They could go to the cinema for three pence on Saturday mornings. They could meet in the shops and parks or go to one of the museums.

I had made a friend of Netty, who came from a family of eight. They originated from Ireland but came to England to allow her father to work in the motor industry. I recall one day when the form mistress asked about our religion; most replied 'Church of England', Netty said 'Roman Catholic', I just said 'Chapel' and a snigger rippled around the classroom.

The list of clothes needed at school included laced shoes for travelling, shoes with a buttoned strap for indoor wear, white gym shoes and one spare pair of lisle stockings to change into if the weather was wet. My mother economised where ever possible and thought that two pairs of stockings were enough. We had clean ones each Sunday. My stockings were never wet when we arrived at school. They had always dried during the train journey.

I wasn't alone in failing to keep those extra stockings. A member of staff stood at the doorway asking each pupil if stockings had been changed. To overcome her question, Netty and I would sit on our boot 'cubby holes', take off our stockings putting them on opposite legs. We had honestly changed our stockings and this situation lasted till the teacher became wise to our antics.

'Will you please show me your wet stockings as you go through the doorway,' she ordered.

One girl who always conformed precisely went past her with her spares, then returned for a forgotten book. She handed us her stockings, we carried one each, so we were successful again. Now we would not have to plead with our mums for an extra pair.

Another source of derision was my nails. I had rough hands, nails worn down and ragged, with often bleeding cuticles. They were the result of weeding, planting and lifting potatoes from dry limestone brash soil.

When the teacher felt like humiliating me she would do a nail inspection. I was forced to put my hands on the desk in full view of the class. My mother carefully explained that I would not need a nail inspection to enter heaven. 'You can judge a person's character by their nails,' she assured me. 'Yours are the nails of hard work – something to be praised.' Mum considered manicured and polished nails were an attempt at personal attraction, and never to be tolerated. Dad just pronounced 'Stinking pride'.

I tended to mix with the sporty girls in the class where the topic of conversation was predictable. 'We are going to see The Wasps tomorrow. Why don't you come?' I was mystified. I had seen plenty of wasps, too many when jam making. I just said, 'No thank you. I'm going to see a football match in the afternoon.' 'Who do you watch?' they asked and quite innocently I said 'Combe.' 'Combe,' they echoed, 'They don't play football – that's soccer.' I'd never heard the word before but after the explanation that The Wasps was a rugby football team, I began to understand. Class distinction again looming its ugly head, even in sport. I soon became accustomed to the 'Quins' and the 'Baa baas'.

A game derived from football, surely it should have changed its name when they decided to carry the ball. As for a ball; my dictionary says a ball is a sphere.

I was learning but not understanding.

At home the market gardening enterprise was blossoming, there was far more work for me and far more money. But never a penny came my way.

15   At home, 1932

Through pressure of homework and waning enthusiasm from Dad, my sister had been forced to give up her music lessons. She had already succeeded in playing the hymns for our morning Sunday school. Our hymns were chosen according to her ability to play them. She always chose 'Immortal Invisible God Only Wise' but we often encouraged her to play 'Lorelei'.

Our elderly superintendent always shed a tear when we sang the verse:

> *Forth into that dreadful battle*
> *The steadfast soldier goes*
> *No friend where he lies dying*
> *His eyes to kiss and close.*

We thought it was so unusual to see a man crying, we actually cruelly set up the situation. Many years later we heard that he had lost his only son in the First World War.

1932 was a very hot year, water was very short and because of the hard bedrock in Stonesfield they had no water at all there. Farmers trundled along with their horse drawn water barrels to the Evenlode, a long haul along the bottom of Dad's grass field. Such daily traffic had worn away the grass and the gate was often left open, so the field could not be used. Friction ensued; should it be water for all, or pasture for one? That one happened to be paying the rent. The debate was never settled until the Lord intervened and sent the rain. The same situation arose again the following year.

Every available hand was used in bringing in the corn harvest. As soon as, or even before, we were old enough all children helped. We were keen; we led the horse from shock to shock[9]. Sometimes we stacked the sheaves on the wagon or tossed them across the rick[12]. I will never forget the insects that accompanied us on the wagon as we rode on the empty trailer to collect another load. There were spiders, crane flies, earwigs and beetles of every size and hue. Those dry straws that had stood so long in the sun offered a snug, cosy home for so many.

During those long summer holidays my sister and I were allocated the job of carrying water to the hens. They were now out in the fields living on the leasings of corn that had avoided the binder. They were free-range hens now in the true meaning of the phrase. The cattle yard at the barn had a very deep well, water was always available but the valve in the pump would not retain its water. The pump was about five feet high, but a can of water was always kept ready to pour into the top. Then, pumping furiously, like Moses we obtained our water. There was a surrounding fence so we used it as a ladder to reach the top. The handle was both too heavy and long for us, but it had to be done.

So with two buckets each we staggered over the fields to the thirsty hens, slopping water into our shoes as we went. The hens pushed and shoved and drank while we returned for more. No feeding was necessary as there was food in abundance. The limestone grit was of little use to them so we gave them flint in one tray for their gizzards and oyster shell grit in another to ensure perfect eggshells.

When working at the farm we had no watch with us, nor any need of one. The Worcester GWR line was clearly visible and very dependable. We knew each train, its speed, its cargo and destination. There was a coal train with identical trucks, we called it 'Dicky Thomas' (Richard Thomas), it carried coal from South Wales to the main stations. There was 'The Pick Up', which carried freight to and from smaller stations including timber from Blenheim saw mill[1]. The brown and cream passenger trains steamed along at frequent intervals.

We could always hear the sirens indicating to the workmen it was time for a rest. There was one from the Witney blanket factory and another from Blenheim. The loudness of the sirens and trains helped us to determine the weather for the near future.

Feast Sunday arrived and after evening service we had a camp meeting outside the chapel. Our own harmonium was used as it was small and had handles and was therefore quite portable. This was an annual occurrence but the previous year it had been disrupted by the Woodstock Brass Band.

Dad decided to be tactful this year, so when all was set up for the service and the band likewise installed by The Cock Inn, he approached the conductor and suggested they came and played the hymns for us. They readily agreed and harmony prevailed again.

Dark evenings approached and homework was becoming a problem. We only had one table in the kitchen-cum-living room so we could not begin until the washing up was finished and packed away – we did not have a village water supply, so naturally no sink.

Mum's sock machine was firmly clamped on one corner of the table. As the handle turned the table shook. That was bad enough, but when she was doing the heels and toes, the machine went forwards and backwards, so both the writing and the concentration suffered. There was one oil table lamp that cast shadow over the table and it was always positioned to benefit Mum.

November arrived, as did the fogs. We always set off as usual even under extreme conditions. The train was late, but unlike many others we did arrive at school. When the fog did not lift all day, too bad for hockey, a thick yellow fog enveloped the world. The head mistress decided to close the school early to allow the girls time to get home; except us of course. We left at the usual time, walking up 'The High' where lights were barely visible. Our train left at 5.30, but we connected with a London train, which was to arrive five minutes earlier. It failed to appear, station announcements continued but there was no hope until about seven o'clock. The first indication that it was coming was the sound of detonators on the track. Our train was prepared, signals could not be seen, so as we depended on detonators, progress was very slow.

Arriving at Hanborough we lit our oil lamps but they neither helped us to see nor to be seen. We travelled slowly up the long road keeping our eyes on the verge. Suddenly that verge disappeared so we got off to establish where we were. We had arrived at the garage so we had missed our turn. We doubled back and approached the long descent to the river. We had to walk, the risk was too great to ride and truthfully we were a bit scared. At the bottom of the hill we met Dad. He had an acetylene lamp on his bike, which was an improvement. His presence made the rest of the journey tolerable. He had not been to work as it was too foggy to plough. We arrived home after nine o'clock.

Rain arrived during the night so we were off to school again at seven-thirty next morning.

16   Humiliation

We went into the sports hall for our midday meal. I called it dinner but the others said lunch. We sat at trestle tables with a plate and a glass of water. I kept my paper bag containing my toast in my satchel on my lap, hoping my meagre meal would not be noticed. But the duty staff dictated that our complete meal should be placed on the plate – good table manners, she insisted.

Oh dear! Mine was in a paper bag that had clearly been used several times, while others had theirs wrapped in greaseproof paper. The queer-shaped dripping toast that I was enjoying was obviously an object of ridicule.

The derision was mutual. Why cut the crusts from bread? What a waste! Hadn't they ever heard of 'Waste not, want not'? One girl showed me exactly how to score an orange to simplify its peeling. She knew that I never ever had an orange.

One day a girl, very proud of her new shoes, talked incessantly about them. 'They cost sixteen and eleven,' she bragged, 'How much did yours cost?' 'Mine were only twelve and eleven,' admitted another, then, the dreaded question, 'How much did yours cost?' directed to me. I just mumbled 'Five and eleven,' but I knew they were three and eleven.

Another topic was hairdressing. I was one of only four in the class that had long hair, so the school rules insisted it should be plaited. 'Friday night is Amami night,' quoted one. 'Do you shampoo yours on Fridays?' This was the first time I had heard the word 'shampoo' so I guessed she meant washing.

'Not always,' I admitted.

'Do you use Amami?' she persisted.

'No,' I confessed, 'I use soap.'

'Soap!' they all exclaimed, 'What sort of soap?'

'I use towel soap,' I muttered guiltily.

'What is towel soap?' they queried. Then, thinking I was giving them a useful tip, I explained that if you kept the empty soap cartons, they could be exchanged for towels. As Mum did lots of washing both for us and for others, we used lots of soap and the family were well blest for towels.

One week everyone appeared to be going out of their way to make my life easier. In other words, I think my situation had been discussed in the staff room. The art teacher, who had always given up on me (and I didn't blame her, I was a logic thinker, certainly not a flicker of design in me) suddenly exclaimed mine was the best drawing. It certainly was not, but it was mounted and pinned onto the wall for all to see. Then, I was told to stand up and they all had to give me a clap. Such humiliation!

The English teacher chose a page from a book which was really a long discussion. For homework we were to rewrite it not using any word from the verb 'to say'. In one place I dropped the word 'said' and inserted 'suggested'. Why was

I called to the front of class and made to read it out? Could it be coincidence? I don't think so because I received another round of applause. Maybe I was naïve, but this was ridiculous; I thought so, and so did the rest of the class.

The attention that I received the following day was much more to my liking. A prefect came into the classroom during registration and asked to speak to me. I knew her well, she was the school cricket captain and I already practised with the school team. 'The Indians are playing in the parks today. I will collect you at a quarter to four and take you to see them.'

This was much too good to miss. I really knew nothing about university cricket except that the visiting country always played their first match in Oxford. I did know that a prince would be playing for India. So I was met and walked to the parks. Now I had seen something the rest of the class had not, and what was more the younger generation from Combe had not seen them either. I began to read the back page of the newspaper.

I became quite friendly with Grace; her father was manager of an iron foundry in Walton Well Road. She took me there one day and we saw molten iron being poured into moulds to make street lamps.

One girl, whose father was a surgeon, arrived at biology class with the skeleton of a hen. I nudged my friend Netty and said, 'Coo, my Mum would make some nice soup with that.' The teacher heard it and gave me a good dressing down. 'Your parents wouldn't dream of doing anything for the benefit of the class,' she said bluntly.

Her statement was probably true, but mine was as well. My mother never wasted even a crumb of bread. You couldn't feed a sparrow on the left-overs at our house.

17   Enjoyment

In spite of all my shortcomings I did enjoy my school days. I excelled in maths including algebra and geometry. Chemistry, physics and biology were just as simple. I kept up with French and geography, and English was improving all the time. My two bogey subjects were Latin and history.

The most enjoyable day was sports day, always on a Saturday. Heats for all races were held beforehand so it was only the finals.

The most important item was not even a race; it was the grand march. We had been practising for weeks. It was compulsory for each pupil to participate. We were lined up on the netball pitch making a very long queue going up and down. We were led by the sixteen prefects, followed by all the school starting with the smallest. We entered the playing field in single file from each side of the Iffley Road hut. We marched in twos, then fours, then eights and then sixteens before starting the casting off and returning to the exact place from which we had come. The City of Oxford Band was always there to play Colonel Bogey and no one was ever out of step. I remember so well seeing those white gym shoes pacing up and down.

As well as sports day we always had a P.E. day. It was held on one of the grass tennis courts. Forms competed against each other and there was an adjudicator to award a cup on completion. We competed both as a form and individually. We jumped horses and did cartwheels, or stood on our hands. Nothing was barred if you had a party piece.

Expanding on this we had inter-form hockey matches. Each form wore its allocated colours as a sash, which showed to all that you were in the team. I was always in the form team, playing centre half.

Another inter-form competition that parents could attend was singing. We had an extremely good singing mistress who chose our songs very wisely. I remember 'Brother James Air' with descants and 'Where 'ere you Walk'. One year it was the tune from *The Planets Suite*, 'I Vow to Thee My Country'. While I was there our adjudicator was always Sir Thomas Beecham. We always did a lot of practice on the hymns to be used at the annual school service held at St Mary's in The High. All city grammar schools attended.

My class sometimes played tricks, especially on certain members of staff. The French teacher who also taught needlework lent herself to such treatment. If she was given flowers, she would plunge her nose deep into the blooms, then go into ecstasies about their beauty. So this group pooled their money and bought her some Parma violets. They left them on her table, but they had been heavily seasoned with pepper. The whole class held their breath and waited, and the result did not disappoint. Her sneezing was so bad that she had to leave the room. On returning she was naturally furious.

'Stand up if you did or had any knowledge of this offence,' she ordered. The whole class stood to attention immediately, except me. I was reluctantly hauled to my feet feeling very guilty. The whole class was reported to the head mistress. After coming to speak to the class she issued the punishment. All of us were to attend detention on Saturday morning. This punishment was usually given to individuals for unfinished homework but as I travelled in from the country I was always excused, as was one other who travelled from Banbury. Late on Friday afternoon the message came through that detention was cancelled.

18   1933 – disruption

Rumours were whispered around the local villages that some chapels were to close. The names Wesleyan, United and Primitive were to be dropped and all chapels would be called just 'Methodist'.

My parents were very attached to the United Methodist in Combe as Dad's grandfather was involved in building it. Dad was a trustee and he wasn't going to give it up without a fight.

This spring the potatoes were ready to be planted as usual during the Easter holidays. Mum however decided against helping; too many gloves and socks to make. There were also lots of bedding plants to be pricked out. We didn't really approve but we just had to obey orders, just the two of us planting now. There was a lot of work in the market gardening enterprise, more than we could do properly. Every available minute was used by every available hand.

I was nearly thirteen and my sister was past fourteen. We had recognised that there was to be a major event in the family. At first we just couldn't believe it, we discussed it each night when we were in bed. Mum was thirty-nine years old, such an event had happened last year in Rose's family. Now we knew why Mum hadn't planted potatoes this year.

When would she tell us – or rather would she ever tell us? It was a taboo subject in our family and the topic was not touched on in school either. We just gleaned our knowledge in those days. We would have to wait. The summer was scorching hot, greenhouses had sprung up in our garden like mushrooms overnight; now, laden with tomatoes and cucumbers, they needed a lot of water. Water had to be pumped; we were on a good spring so really very lucky. But buckets of water are heavy and Mum was directing the job to us, the girls again. My own birthday came and went, the corn was ripening very early because of the heat wave. We were still attending chapel, but it looked now that it would close on August 27. We had the last camp meeting outside the chapel on feast Sunday with Woodstock Band in attendance. Due to the heat the potatoes also ripened very early – like the corn, a very poor crop and an extremely early harvest.

The Stonesfield farmers' water barrels were still trundling along Dad's field, collecting that vital element of life, but that unseen brotherhood that built up over the years between farmers was being severely tested and strained. It was very noticeable when we went to Stonesfield feast camp meeting. It was undetectable while we were singing hymns accompanied by the Salvation Army band, or even praying with one voice for rain, but those little pow-wows and discussions that usually followed such meetings were missing. It appeared that Dad was being avoided.

Rumours were spreading like wildfire, however, that piped water would soon be coming to both Stonesfield and Combe. I wondered then if the collective thanks for pumped water would be as fervent and intense as their pleas for rain were now.

Our cosy, pampered home life was to face this upheaval, likewise our religious life. Expectancy hung over each member of the family but was never ever shared. We were meant to be aloof to all that was buzzing around us. We were not meant to notice Mum's struggle home from Stonesfield camp meeting that year.

August 27 at last approached. We attended each service as always, we prayed for our own future. Conversation revolved around where we would be the following Sunday. My parents did not participate, I think because of Mum's situation; but I sensed that Dad was hurt and there was a bit of revenge in his attitude. He did not have to divulge his future master plan, perhaps he didn't even have one. We gleaned nothing from his outward appearance.

We sang a few hymns after the last service, one was 'The day Thou Gavest' but on our knees we finished with 'Abide with Me'. Many a tear splashed on to the floor, emotions were high but hands were shaken, best wishes were being strewn around like confetti. Never again would we read that text over the pulpit, 'Enter into his courts with praise and into his gates with thanksgiving'.

It was over; praying both for rain and the chapel had produced no outward effect. The following Sunday I went to the village church with Rose – that was her family's chosen bent. She would at least know when to stand or sit or kneel. Now I would be able to make use of the prayer book items I had learnt at primary school.

It was straight back to work the following day, the last day of the potato harvest. Work would still carry on; we had onions, carrots, turnips and beet-root to harvest now. They would each go into their individual clamp[8] to keep ready for sale during the winter. Mum rose very early that day, it was washday and with so much washing to do for all her customers she was buoyant. Among all the towels and pillowcases she washed, dried and ironed were thirteen sheets.

The sun scorched down on us all, the ground was hot and parched. It was about six o'clock that evening that Mum called over the wall to our neighbour. We were all on the farm with Dad. Ted, next door, was sent to fetch Dad. We were excited as we knew exactly what was happening.We finished picking up potatoes and Ted covered the clamp with straw and soil. We cycled home, but were met at the gate by Dad, who diverted us to Gran's house just down the road. Still no explanation, then about nine-thirty Dad appeared to give us the news. 'You'll never guess what we've got at home,' he proclaimed, 'You've got a baby sister!' Surprise, surprise! Did he really think that we were so dim-witted or unobservant? – but they had kept up their mysterious, invisible curtain to the end.

I personally was delighted, I wanted it to be a girl. I loved babies, but I never dreamed that we would be lucky enough to have one. There was already a maternal instinct lurking in my character.

That Christmas we were going to walk to Freeland as usual for the midday meal. Other years we had all walked across the meadows and up the hill to the Freeland turn. We called that block of red brick buildings 'the red city'. This year there was a pram to push so I offered to walk the long way round up Swan Hill and along the Witney road. There was no danger, very little traffic and certainly no footpaths.

This was a responsibility I relished. It was cementing my desire for a family as opposed to a career.

19   Village life

Combe with 429 residents (in 1921) was a quiet, restful village, its small cottages nestled around the green, and that in turn encouraged so much activity. The cows crossed and re-crossed it as they went from field to farm. They needed no herdsman, they knew the way and they tended to amble along choosing their own pace.

The old oak tree, protected by railings, had seen centuries of village life, children played cricket around it, the village bonfire blazed away in November and each year May day brought the maypole. The chapel enthusiasts once carried their banners around it on Easter Sunday, but alas, no more. The fair with their horse drawn vehicles filled the green on feast Sunday and this year the annual camp meeting was going to take place near the war memorial.

There were three pubs around the green and three shops. The church dominated one corner.

The sports field was only a few yards away – it just concentrated on cricket. Every lad in the village aspired to become a cricketer. This was not achieved easily; it took years of practice even when you were in the team. Those nets by the pavilion were always in use. This devotion to cricket produced, during the coming years, the best village cricket team in the country. There were evening matches adding to the dedication to the sport. That so-called 'holy square' was nursed and coddled to perfection. It was however left deserted and abandoned on Sundays. Several of the cricketers were teetotallers and would take either bottles of milk or water to away matches in spite of the ridicule they received.

Near the green was the coffee tavern, always an asset to the village although now diverted from its original use. It was given as a present to the village to encourage lads to read and play games rather than walk the roads or frequent the pubs. Females were not allowed inside. The occupant at this time was a Mr Gibson. He was a sociable character who had lost a leg during the war. He had a war pension and living at the coffee house gave him a home with no rent, free fuel and a social life. He also was a cricket enthusiast, so he slotted into the role of umpire. He was ideally suited to the village and his function in it. He was also a churchwarden.

Sunday was a nothing day for the lads, no sport, no work, no shopping – only church or chapel, but most of them did attend one place of worship on Sunday evening. They would congregate by the main village shop after Sunday roast. There were usually between ten and twenty of them. They walked towards Hanborough railway station. They appeared to take no interest in girls.

Conversation varied from cricket to politics and back to cricket again. They each carried a walking stick – it was the style of the moment. Tip-tap went those sticks; they could be heard a long way off.

I recall one Sunday, I went to my uncle's for the midday meal. He had one son at least ten years my senior who had been to the lads' meeting spot that morning, and without either of his parents or the shop owner knowing, he had bought a packet of sweets from the shop owner's son. This was Sunday, and how my uncle knew I do not know, but he did know before my cousin arrived home. The rest of the sweets were taken from him and thrown into the fire. That meal was awful, the tension gripped the family. I did not speak, I just thought 'what a waste'.

20   Modernisation

In the years between 1930 and 1935 Combe was leaping into the future.

It was the start of digging up roads and wires criss-crossing above us. Six new council houses were built in Akeman Street and although each pair had a well, it would soon be made redundant. Electricity came first carried on overhead lines; then water which came in pipes laid underground.

Some were welcoming these arrivals but many were predetermining the cost. 'We don't want electricity,' said my Dad, 'We don't understand it.'

Dad had always taken charge of light in the house. He would blow out the lamp very early to make doubly sure that the family did not spend too much on paraffin. Electricity was very different; a bill would accumulate and he would have no control. We did not need it for cooking purposes as the farm produced massive amounts of wood. He stood firm and we did not get its benefit when it first came to the village. The company offered, as far as I can remember, three lights and one point for one pound. He would not budge and Mum was quietly seething; she would benefit, as would the rest of us.

The last straw came one Monday evening when she had gone to Women's Institute. I was left at home looking after Marion (my young sister) while doing my homework. Dad was sitting in his chair with his feet as usual on the mantle piece. A knock on the door proved to be Mr. Walter Green. I think they were talking about taking sugar beet to the station. They stood talking with the door open for some time, while the fire was gradually going out. Marion was colouring a book, sitting in her high chair at the table. The paraffin lamp was standing on a crocheted mat. She reached out and pulled the mat, the lamp fell over and broke, paraffin splashed everywhere. It was both dark and cold.

At that moment Mum came home and although she was seldom flustered, that night altered everything. She was furious. 'Now I shall have my way,' she stamped, 'I shall call in the electricity company this week. I will never buy another paraffin lamp.'

Mum was now boss as far as electricity was concerned. We had three lights downstairs and an electric kettle was ordered. No lights upstairs, where we still used candles.

Dad dug in his heels again when piped water arrived. 'We've always got clean cold water, easily pumped.' This time he was right, as the stream that supplied us with water had trickled through limestone and often friends would call just to beg a glass full. They did not install mains water until after I was married.

I had settled into going to the church with Rose and very soon we were invited to join the church choir. Mum and Dad now went to church but took turns in staying at home with Marion. We went to confirmation classes that winter, and on St. Patrick's Day several of us were confirmed in Christ Church cathedral.

The church Sunday school and choir went on a day trip that year to Whipsnade Zoo, and we really did enjoy it.

Life in an Oxfordshire village was beginning to expand.

21 Uniform

Our uniform at Milham Ford School was respected by some and ridiculed by many. It was based on navy blue and white. If you saw a girl with plaits – as a few of us still had – you would be excused if you had thought we went to St Trinian's.

The gymslip was the usual one with three pleats both front and back. We wore a white girdle knotted like a tie. The length of the skirt varied – some liked the shortest possible and some erred the other way. Miss Lamb, our sports mistress, often descended on us and dictated the length with a tape measure. We knelt on the floor of the gymnasium and the length should be exactly four inches from the ground. This is rather short, but some mums had bought gymslips that were too long, expecting their daughters to grow into them.

Of course whatever we wore underneath was often on view. The most difficult aspect was making sure there was no gap around our thighs. It was the days of stockings sometimes clutched by suspenders, often supplemented by garters. We had those lovely, warm gym knickers with long legs and a pocket. If the legs were pulled down that would easily have prevented the gap. For the sake of comfort we always yanked up the legs, this ensured that those lisle stockings were stretched to the limit. Both slips and stockings were dispensed with in gym lessons.

We did lots of apparatus work and I revelled in it. Outdoor shoes had to be black laced, while indoor shoes worn at school must have a strap and button. We always kept our white gym shoes at school.

We wore long navy coats in the winter and navy velour hats with a brim. A brighter blue hatband encircled it with M.F.S. in the front. We were obliged to wear navy blue gloves both winter and summer. In summer we had a lighter blue cotton dress, to be made with specified material and pattern. Legs must still be kept covered by those awful stockings. We had navy blazers edged with a lighter blue braid. All parts of the uniform were purchased from Webbers.

It was our summer hats that caused the sensation. They were white straw boaters with the usual hatband stating to the world that we belonged to M.F.S. We always called these hats 'bashers'. Although they were originally white, the sun tanned and mellowed them. My own hat had an elastic chinstrap, which was essential when cycling to the station.

We loved them, but the newly appointed head mistress soon decided to rid the school of such monstrosities. Nearly four hundred girls decided differently; many of the parents of paying pupils had chosen this school because of the hat, for when in a public place we always stood out in a crowd. This ensured that behaviour could not be extreme. So, after many form meetings and letters to the head, she conceded and promised not to change the hat without first a vote of the whole school.

She stood no chance, and that hat was still in use long after I left.

I have seen those hats often misused. One girl, who was afraid of a cricket ball, was fielding in the deep, and as the ball came towards her she whipped off her hat to catch it. She caught the ball but it went straight through the hat.

I heard of several city scholars floating them down the Isis while boys tried to sink them with marbles. I saw many letters hidden in the inside band, taken out quickly and popped through the Magdalen College fence.

Did you receive any in that way, Geoffrey?

Who would dispose of such a multipurpose item of clothing? I loved my basher, I still have it after sixty-five years...

22   Two kinds of Labour

School was going well, I was now fourteen and already playing in both the hockey and netball teams. The latter always had two goal scorers and those two places were taken by my friend Netty and myself. We would practise shooting every possible minute, spending many dinner hours there and becoming very skilful. Netty did not usually play hockey but I always played centre half and left back. Behind me was Grace. She was good – I don't think I was too bad either.

There was soon to be a national election. This was a topic that I knew quite a lot about. We were to have a mock election at school. Candidates were adopted, then Netty and I went to the assembly hall to listen to speeches. Our

Voting, originally a privilege, was now a birthright. We were taught to use it and not abuse it. I think our mock election took place in the year that women were given the full franchise, and I well remember my mother voting for the first time.

minds were made up; we would vote for the Labour candidate, namely Olive Cox (who later became Olive Gibbs). I think we must have heard her first political speech. She had no chance of winning when about seventy per cent of all pupils came from families who paid for the education of their offspring.

I often wonder about the effect that this mock election had. Olive went on to work hard for the council and Netty's brother worked hard for the union at the motor works.

The previous mock election had never been forgotten. Miss McCabe was headmistress at the time. She was confined to a wheelchair by arthritis but was still severe and unapproachable. She dictated that everyone should vote; 'decisions, decisions, decisions' was instilled in us. Women had been given the vote in 1928, just a few years earlier. We were taught about 'free trade', 'the gold standard' and other topics which most of us failed to understand. 'You cannot make laws but you do have the chance to vote in a government that can.'

The sixth formers realised that Miss McCabe was the only non-voter. That must change. They found Griffiths – he was the caretaker and manual workers were only addressed by their surname – and he lent them his wheelbarrow, which they decorated with blue ribbons and rosettes. She protested but the pupils were young and strong and determined. The result was the oddest spectacle. I wouldn't think that it helped her arthritis.

During the early thirties England dominated the tennis world. I think Fred Perry won the men's singles at Wimbledon each year. For Oxford fans the boat race was very different, I think Oxford lost each year. These were the topics that manipulated our conversations. I really did have to read 'the back page' now. When it came to The Grand National I knew nothing, as horses, which encouraged betting, were never even mentioned in the household.

Our journeys to and from school were being controlled by mum. The Institute stall had moved to the Oxford covered market now and opened two days a week on Wednesdays and Fridays. There was always a car from Combe on Wednesdays, mum took her turn at helping and the car took her produce. Friday was different, no car, but they needed her produce and she needed to sell it. Bags of stuff were hung on our handlebars and we had to take them into our carriage, amid comments and jokes, and from Oxford station we carried them as far as number four avenue in the market. This really was the limit, what with books as well it was not safe on the bicycle and far too heavy when walking. We were forced into doing it and reluctantly we just did.

Returning from school was similar. There was a Butler's corner shop in Park End Street that sold goods cheaper than anywhere else. Their Oxos were seven for sixpence when other shops were one penny each. They had broken biscuits for three pence a pound, their buns were in my estimation very good and well cooked and certainly the cheapest.

Just down the road at the entrance to Oxpens was a cheerful old lady selling bananas from a pushcart. She was always there on Wednesdays and as it was the end of the day she would offer us a bag full for three pence.

But the worst shopping was from Curtis and Horn. They were agricultural specialists in Park End Street. If anything was needed for the farm, nails, nuts and bolts and often shot gun cartridges, we collected them. It was always something very heavy. My sister and I always argued about the shopping, but as she was older she always won.

This was the year that Marks and Spencer opened its five-shilling store in Oxford. It was very different from Woolworths that sold nothing over sixpence. If we needed any item of clothing, however, we were sent to Cape's in St. Ebbe's where the bill and money was sprung overhead by some unseen force to the central office. It usually returned with your change, receipt and a farthing change in pins.

23   Better be born lucky than rich

1935 brought changes. My sister was taking her school certificate. She was nervous and worried but we just endured her.

The long expected railway halt was to open at Combe. It would eliminate cycling to Hanborough but as my sister was leaving school this year she would have little benefit. The date was set at July 8th, which was in the same week that Fred Perry won his last Wimbledon championship. It was a big day for Combe. The village now had a workman's bus early each morning and a shopper's bus on Wednesdays and Saturdays and now stopping trains to Oxford and indeed fast trains to Paddington.

Leaving school that July my sister soon got a job as secretary at Burton's dairies. She clocked off each milkman as he returned from his morning round.

In the train compartment we had one extra occupant. She was already on the train when it arrived at the halt. She was dressed in a green uniform and clearly going to Wychwood School. My first impression was of a formidable, attractive female with a polished accent. Her name was Deborah Mitford. She had obviously been deprived of school friends because, like a clock spring winding down, she just kept talking. Maybe it was nerves or excitement but I do not think so. She usually had a chaperon, either a nanny or her mother.

Her topics of conversation were wasted on us, coming out balls and the wide world beyond, scenes that we had never and would never witness.

I did not covet her life style; I thought it was boring, it meant nothing to me. If we were quiet and did not enter into her deliberations, she would embark on an irritating, consistent moan about the imposition of wearing a uniform. She hated it; it was the first time she had attended school although she was probably sixteen or seventeen. I wore my uniform with pride but she had no respect at all for hers. One day she rolled down the carriage window and threw out her hat. That was one item gone for ever. Her mother just smiled.

The escapades of Deborah's older sisters were filtering into the headlines of the papers. This notoriety increased rapidly in the next few years. Deborah shone through her family's notoriety.

In my position, I could not have attended school without a uniform. I took care of it, always taking it off when I arrived home. It was indeed worth more than any other clothes I had.

At school this was my certificate year but, as we started that September, we were given the tragic news of Netty's family. Tuberculosis had attacked and she had lost her father, eldest sister and youngest brother. She was in no fit state to attend school but she did. Her religion was clearly helping her. She unloaded the sad story on me, and she couldn't stop talking about her youngest brother. I had met her family so I knew him and could sympathise.

Netty and I had much in common, and proudly wore our red girdles which announced to the whole school that we were representing them. But it was not a good year for sport, the English weather so often intervened. The cricket matches suffered the same fate.

She was now the second oldest in her family and knew, for financial reasons, her education must finish in July.

Together we would help each other with revision. We would repeat French and Latin verbs until they haunted us like melodies. Netty always outshone me in English but not so in Maths. She vowed she would not pass; but she did. In those days you either passed or failed the whole exam. No passes for individual subjects. A complete pass needed at least five individual passes. They included English, maths, one foreign language plus two other subjects. We waited with trepidation in the corridors of the examination schools. The huge T-shaped room was frightening. All the Oxford schools were there, most still chanting verbs or repeating a passage of Latin. Our examination results would determine our futures. The results would be known towards the end of August, so my future was not seriously discussed until then. Our class did extremely well that year including both Netty and myself. My own passes were nearly all As, but Latin and history let me down. No surprise there.

On the last day of my school life we queued outside the office of the head mistress to say goodbye and thank her.

I had well rehearsed my small speech but, shaking hands, she spoke first: 'What have you planned to do with your life?' Before I could answer, she did: 'I suppose you will find a pen-pushing job until you get married.'

I was deflated, as clearly she thought I was a failure. I only found out later that most of us had been treated the same.

We were leaving school and more than a little excited. 'Career or family', my intentions were still being balanced on the scales but family was still winning.

24   The wide, wide world

Now, at the age of sixteen, I was free for harvest. I liked that carefree outside existence but I really thought that I should receive some remuneration. Nothing forthcoming, I was told that I was having my board and lodging and should be grateful. The only pocket money I ever had was the occasional halfpenny to buy a yellow sherbet dab.

I was beginning to realise that there were times in one's own life when one had to make one's own decisions. My intentions were not to be overruled this time. I did not consider going to work – or even for an interview – with two long heavy plaits. I spent the first morning of my free life cycling to the barbers in Woodstock.

'Do you want to keep your plaits as a keepsake?' he said.

'No!' I answered emphatically.

He carefully explained that they were worth quite a bit, so he gave me an address, and a few days later I received just over two pounds.

I wouldn't be quite so poor this summer. Combe Feast came and I would enjoy myself. I gave Marion several rides and an ice cream, then Mum came and collected her at eight. 'You can stay until half past nine,' limiting me because she wanted to avoid a collision with Dad. I soon located Rose and Dorothy and we all took a ride on the Cake Walk. When that was over and we had had our laughs, several boys chased us with squibs.[11] We all pretended it was horrible, but in all fairness the enjoyment was mutual. I arrived home at the dictated time, but, some kind friend had spilled the beans about my dreadful deeds. Villages were like that, news travelled faster then than it does now on a mobile phone.

Dad had often shown his disgust at the Cake Walk, and now his own daughter had joined in the fun. I was sent straight to bed, but Marion slept with me now so there was little he could do without waking her. I opened the window and the fair organ could be heard in the distance until midnight.

During the summer we cycled back from the farm very late. Mum went first taking Marion and preparing a substantial meal for all. My brother, now fourteen, took the horses to the field. I cycled home with Dad. Tired as we both were, I recall him walking with me just to count the glowworms. We listened to the corncrakes and nightjars.

I recall him telling me the benefits of both jackdaws and lapwings. They ate snails and insects, but rooks and crows were on the other side of the fence and should be eliminated. Those bleak fields were the habitat of grey partridges. We saw the occasional French red-legged one and thought how lucky we were.

In the spring the gamekeeper walked those fields of growing corn spacing out thorny twigs to irritate the poachers. Partridge poachers used large nets and when a covey was disturbed they were all caught together. Those thorny twigs were expected to ruin their nets.

Overnight my father's anger and wrath had been changed to amiable harmony. I wondered why. Perhaps my mother coaxed him or even dominated him. If so, I belatedly thank her; but wonder if my hours of energy that were given buckshee had any influence.

I knew I was still naïve, my family were too narrow and work orientated. I never ever remember either of my parents going to a cinema or theatre. That pleasure was wicked. We had no radio. When Dad sat down in the dark evenings, he would put his feet on the table or mantelpiece, stick a self-rolled cigarette in his mouth and read the newspaper. If Marion was becoming a nuisance at bedtime, he would nurse her to sleep, or rather they would fall asleep together. Ashes from his cigarette would drift over her.

On warm summer evenings it was my job to coax her to sleep. I had to lie in my mother's bed and sing to her, poor child – then when I thought she was asleep, I would wriggle out of the bed without disturbing her. Sometimes it didn't work and I had to start again. I really adored her and helped to spoil her. I still honestly think that her arrival was the best event ever in the family.

The examination results came, pleasing us all, and now my future could be considered. With Mum escorting me I went to the education offices for advice. We met the same man who had offered me my scholarship five years earlier. I would have considered teacher training but that meant two years away from home. Although training would be free, my parents could not afford it as the work I was doing, especially on Saturdays, would be lost.

But there was a second way into teaching, which was by two years student teaching. This was readily agreed, and I would still be getting quite long holidays and plenty of time to work on the gardening venture.

My annual pay was £24, that was £2 each month but there were some deductions and I finished with £1 16s 8d. Mum took £1 for food and the rest I had for clothes, recreation and transport.

I was posted to Kiddington, just seven miles away, so it was considered quite an easy cycling distance. A very small school but the teacher had demanded help because of the wide age range.

The head mistress, Mrs Checkley – was one of the kindest people I had ever met. She had three boys and no husband, so money had to go a long way. I was sent up to the phone kiosk to put money on a horse. I had definite objections, but I did it, never mentioning it at home. In my ignorance I did not always understand her orders. I always did the playground duty but so many jobs I did had no bearing on teaching. I mixed the Horlicks for the mid-morning break, a free drink at that time. The Horlicks firm provided a large copper jug and plunger. I hated that smell, but after a few years I was drinking it at home and enjoying it. It must have been an acquired taste that needed some perseverance.

The money to finance the school came by monthly cheque which when cashed was divided between four of us: the head teacher, the caretaker, the lavatory attendant and myself. As soon as the cheque arrived I was sent to Chipping Norton to cash it. I had never been on a double-decker bus before or even bought a bus ticket, nor had I ever been either to Chipping Norton or a bank. That was my assignment so, with trepidation, I did it. Worse was to follow, 'When you have the money, pop into Petiphers and buy a bottle of port.'

Against my principles again but it had to be done.

The situation at school was beginning to dawn on me. Mrs Checkley often took a few minutes off to go into the house. Could that be the resulting smell that I had not recognised? She did have the occasional cigarette but never in the classroom or during school hours. Her smoking did not play havoc with my cough as Dad's did.

She insisted on bringing me a warm bowl of soup at lunchtime. It was very acceptable but it was made with a soup cube, it was crumbled and brought to the boil. I didn't tell Mum because her soup was always made with homegrown vegetables, therefore costing nothing. I'm sure she would have disapproved.

In her generosity, she gave me two full-length dance gowns as her dancing days were over. I rolled them up in a paper bag and hid them under my bed. I could not even mention dancing under our roof.

When her garden needed digging she would take all the children and send me out to dig. That was home from home for me. What else would a student teacher do?

I recollect one Friday when a six-year-old girl in my group was very poorly. She was a gamekeeper's daughter who lived in the centre of Glympton woods. Mrs Checkley soon decided what to do. 'Take her home now on your bicycle, her sister was ill last year and I allowed her to go home on the bus. She died of appendicitis later that day.' The teacher was very concerned, but this year she had me there to help. I had already met the family, who had escorted me around the woods when the wild daffodils were in bloom. I thought the child was very poorly although her mother did not seem concerned. She too died the following day of diphtheria.

The children at Kiddington school were gleaned from a very wide agricultural area. Scattered farms produced a few pupils but most of the farm labourers lived in tied cottages and they did not settle for long. Such nomadic families brought down the standard in schools. One farmer in Glympton produced mostly vegetables, which gave much seasonal work for women and children. School attendance suffered and the attendance officer often called on them. Then, for a week or two, they would return to school, their heads alive with fleas and their bodies covered with impetigo.

Next came the health visitor. She always treated them at school, as she could not afford the time to locate their mothers in the fields. As soon as the afflictions were overcome the next crop of peas was ready and the vicious circle continued.

In spite of all the drawbacks, my sister Florence had now entered teaching and had settled in at Freeland school.

25   The year of deceit

Winters appeared to be getting colder, in 1928 the Blenheim lake had ice strong enough to allow skating for the whole of February. It has been as severe several times since. This winter the meadows were flooded when the temperature dropped suddenly, there was an expanse of ice and each evening, when skaters had gone home the farmer at Hanborough mill flooded the field again and the ice became thicker. This situation occurred again and again and even the poorest families were buying skates. The skating made a booming noise as the floods had already receded so that there was a space under the ice.

That spring my father had a potato clamp[8] left untouched. At that time there was no marketing board so the acreage of potatoes planted was unknown. The weight of potatoes left on farms could not be counted. When we reached April or May, the country would either have an unsaleable glut or a shortage of high-priced spuds.

One day towards the end of April, Mr Delnevo came from Witney, anxious to buy for his fish and chip outlets. He offered my father £1.10.0 per ton, that is a whole sack full for one shilling and sixpence. They stepped the clamp to esti-mate the weight of potatoes and Dad took the offer. At least he would now have some reward for growing them, and those same willing non-paid hands would have to sort and weigh them.

Soon after Mr Delnevo left, Mr Hick's lorry was seen heading for the farm. 'No potatoes left in the country,' he said, 'I'll buy your clamp. I'll give you £8.7.6 a ton.'

What a difference! Enough to pay the farm rent.

Dad fetched a tarpaulin sheet and erected it around us. Even we were valu-able now, we must keep warm and well until all the potatoes had left the farm. Mr Delnevo and Dad had only stepped the clamp and estimated the tonnage. There could be frosted ones and bad ones so every available sack must be concealed and, mysteriously and in secrecy, hidden in the barn.

Like a child giving round sweets, one for you and one for you, we allocated the sacks of potatoes; one for Mr Delnevo and one for Mr Hicks. This was the first time I had known my father do anything that was underhand. He had sold all the potatoes to Mr Delnevo but surely Mr Delnevo must have known that potatoes were in very short supply. I agreed with Dad and helped him to hide every possible sack of potatoes.

On leaving school I had started to play tennis at the local farm. They encour-aged locals who had a racket to go to the farm to play. I had a racket – a very old fashioned one I had bought from a jumble sale for three pence. This was the only game I did not play at school yet the only one I could play now.

I wanted some shorts so I saved every possible penny to buy material to make some. The material was sixpence a yard and Mum lent me her machine. I was really proud of them, they were pleated and I confess rather short. 'Don't you dare let your Dad see you in those,' Mum thundered, 'Never, never, never.'

So when Dad was home, I always put my gabardine mac over my shorts before cycling off to the farm. When out of sight of the house, I took off my gabardine, rolled it up and put it in my bicycle basket. On returning I did the whole thing in reverse, but I was proud of those shorts and I'm sure I played better wearing them.

During the school year I attended several local schools, a fortnight at Stonesfield, a fortnight at Charlbury infants then back to Kiddington. I was enjoying the work but clearly was not very able because I did not take any responsibility. At last I knew where I was heading.

26   Waking up

As 1938 came in I was still enjoying my choir singing with Rose and another Dorothy. There were plenty of Dorothys around, even Rose was Dorothy Rose, but the Dorothy was dropped to cause less confusion.

Political news now headed every newspaper. Oswald Mosley was touring the country. The Mitford sisters were in the limelight. The international situation was strained and crumbling. Hitler's power was increasing. We now had a radio at home and it was booming out the news whenever Dad was at home. Any other programme was 'a waste of electricity'. I remember the radio had both a large dry battery and a wet accumulator.

I was still at Kiddington but on July 1st I was to be given the status of uncertificated schoolteacher. I was anticipating a much larger wage packet, as I would not be doing so much unpaid work.

The local teacher at Combe and her assistant had bought new cars. Ruth Walker had given hers to her uncle on condition he drove her everywhere she wanted to go. The cars were Morris 8s that were being produced at Cowley. The teachers were arranging a holiday in Scotland visiting the Empire exhibition in Glasgow. Ruth's car would only have two occupants, so she offered me a seat with all expenses paid. She knew I had no money, had never had a holiday, or even been outside Oxfordshire. I grabbed the chance. I was too green at the time to understand the significance of her statement when she admitted that she did not want to travel alone with her widowed uncle. I just wondered why. What a price she paid to get such a holiday! He did share in the cost of petrol.

After attending communion at 'St Phil and James' at the top of Leckford Road we set off for Scotland. We did not stop on the way north till we reached Gretna Green – some three hundred miles. We stayed in the marriage hotel and left for Glasgow the following morning. I was very impressed with the exhibition, where I remember well the tropical section. We carried on passed Loch Lomond, then to Edinburgh. After visiting the castle, we progressed down the Royal Mile to Holyrood Palace. We stayed in Princes Street for two nights, visited the Forth Bridge then toured the Trossachs before returning home.

What a holiday!

A pageant was held in Woodstock to raise money for a new secondary school. All villages in the catchment area were invited to participate. Combe combined with Stonesfield and Bladon to depict the reign of Charles the Second. I recall Nell Gwynne selling oranges, courtiers and lords, but we, coming from Combe, carried in a maypole and danced around it. The pageant was performed for several days on the front lawn of Blenheim.

After one performance we listened to the Salvation Army band in the park. Many lads were poking fun at them and I was disgusted. My upbringing told me to walk away and so did one lad. I really wanted to hear the band but I refused to listen to such ridicule.

We returned home each night on a coach supplied on contract. I had noticed one man keeping close to me as we left the coach. One night he pounced on me and I reacted vehemently. He was lucky if he arrived home without scratches and bruises. I walked home casually and said nothing to my parents but I was waking up to realities. A few days later I was sent to pay a bill for poultry food. That man also attacked me and he received the same treatment. After that I refused to pay any more bills for Dad. I didn't give any reason.

On July 1st I was confirmed as teacher and continued at the same school. My wages rose to £97.10.0 per year, which sounds very little but it was more than local men were earning. Superannuation was now deducted, my mother took £1 per week, but at last I had money both to save and spend.

My first purchase was a piano and music lessons.

That September, after harvest, my father was ill for a few weeks. He had shingles and for a few months he gave up smoking. It was during his illness that Neville Chamberlain came home from Germany waving a scrap of paper that said 'Peace in our time'. Trust in Germany was now at its lowest ebb.

Very late that summer I went to tennis, the summer was hanging on, so the threepenny racket was used again. I walked home pushing my bike and talking to a local lad. But I had overstepped my time limit. As I entered the house Dad grabbed my racket, then said, 'I shall hide this racket, you'll not have it again this year.' I went straight to bed to avoid his temper. I didn't need the racket as it was the end of the season and I could, if needed, always borrow one at the farm. By next year I would have money to spend, and my next purchase would be a Slazenger racket. I never knew what happened to the threepenny racket.

27   Into war

I had already joined the Women's Institute and was also going to a social evening each week at the school house. The two teachers were teaching whist to a few of us. We had about three tables and unlike my parents saw nothing wrong.

Mrs Checkley retired from teaching at Christmas and a new head mistress was appointed. Miss Dobinson was very severe and although she had been teaching for many years she still did not understand children. She used the cane and was clearly going to bring discipline to the school.

I recall a reputable woman walking down the road one day when she met a few children leaving school. Her small dog ran to the children and they stroked it. She immediately went into school and complained that the children had spoken to the dog before speaking to her. They received lines to be done at home. I have always remembered this episode because if that was what a career in teaching meant I certainly didn't want to join it. Those scales were heavily swinging towards a family now.

Although this winter was quite cold, I never stayed away from school because of the weather. Several times the road was very slippery so I walked, pushing my bike, and was able to ride home in the afternoon. My mother had a nasty spell of bronchitis. Now I was obliged to help with housework. I took out the ashes each morning and on Fridays I took up the coconut matting, swept up the dust and washed the flags underneath. I vowed I would never buy such floor covering. This meant getting up earlier before I went to Kiddington.

I was saving well now. A new racket and a week's holiday in August was the aim. Dorothy and I booked the holiday quite early – one week bed and breakfast in Portsmouth at a cost of £5.

We enjoyed our holiday – rumours of war were increasing – but as teenagers I don't think we worried about it. Little did we know that our carefree lives would be shattered forever.

The international situation was coming to the boil, and that spring the government introduced conscription. All twenty-year-olds were called up for service, they were the militia. Then the nineteen- and twenty-one-year-olds were mobilised and, yes, my mother was quite right, we would both have gone if we had been boys.

'Blackout' descended on us for six years, sirens howled around and many evacuees would soon arrive. The nation had changed overnight.

All sport in the village was abandoned, you only did things that were necessary, but everyone pulled their weight. The country worked as one large family. I have always got a kick from any teamwork – maybe a family or sports team. This was teamwork at its best. Some who had empty beds welcomed the evacuees, some – especially the men – joined the A.R.P. I joined the Rest Centre Service, became a National Savings Agent and joined the W.V.S. Politics were abandoned. Everyone who was well and strong enough went to first aid classes.

Apart from when he made his bread deliveries to my home, I think it was there that I first met my husband . Being ten years my senior our paths seldom crossed. Now we both thought that as we should not be needed in battle, we were equally determined to do our best in civvies.

Joining the Rest Centre Service meant that when the air raid warning sounded, we took turns to go to the tavern until the 'all clear'. Frank, my future husband, was walking the fields with a shotgun watching out for 'the Huns'.

I tramped the stretch of houses from the school right to East End selling National Saving Stamps at 6d each and shaking a Red Cross tin to accept everyone's weekly penny.

At Kiddington the school numbers had doubled and we had one extra teacher. I had my class in an adjacent room that had previously acted as a store-room. That was much preferred to two teachers sharing one room. I did not really enjoy these few years at Kiddington as I considered I could teach more efficiently if, first, I was left alone and secondly, if I was not continually prodded into being more rigid and strict.

January 1940 was very cold, snow lay on the ground for weeks and my brother Jim lay in bed with pneumonia. He was sleeping on the landing as indeed he had for some time. The doctor was called, he diagnosed his trouble and gave him two 'M and B' tablets. 'No need to worry,' he said, 'they will cure him.' His temperature subsided, then rapidly increased again. It had entered his other lung. He had a repeat prescription but worse was to follow, he had throm-bosis in his groin. Had that blood clot moved, he would have been dead immediately. So strict orders were given, he must not move or be moved for a month. He could not even have a change of bedclothes.

He survived and on Good Friday he descended the stairs again. Capillary tubes were now being forced into doing the work of the main vein, and he would live with that all his life.

Farm work was well behind this season so the first tractor arrived on the farm, a Fordson with heavy cleats on the wheels.

We could now attend church again together but evensong was at 3 pm to avoid trying to black out the church.

28   Occupations in wartime

The nation's knitting needles were clicking furiously, producing socks and balaclavas. Slogans and posters appeared, telling us to 'dig for victory' or that 'walls have ears' or 'be like Dad, keep Mum'. Iron railings and gates were collected to help the effort. Holidays were on hold until the end of the war.

During the daylight hours there were more important occupations. I took on one allotment although my time was limited.

The old chapel that had closed six years earlier was standing empty, so the women's institute started a jam making enterprise. We bought any spare fruit and sat stirring over our primus stoves. This was a well-organised effort; we were allocated sugar but every jar of jam was sold to shops and thence to the public using their coupons. We used plums, damsons, blackberries, apples and rhubarb – not one fruit was wasted.

Jim kept tame rabbits to sell for human consumption. He chose Flemish giants – what giants they were! I copied him, collecting hay from the roadsides or from under the hedges. In the autumn I went to Blenheim collecting falling acorns for the rabbits to eat. Our rabbits were profitable but so lovable that parting with them seemed cruel. All wars are cruel.

We would spend one Saturday collecting rose hips to make syrup for babies.

During our five-week summer holiday we, the teachers, were drafted back for the middle three weeks. This was to prevent the evacuees from being a nuisance to their benevolent hosts. We were asked to find occupations for them – games, walks, crafts or competitions.

April saw the first call up of women. I was in the first age group to sign on with Rose. Rose was drafted to a munitions factory, while I was told to stay exactly where I was. About a week later Rose returned home. I think her character rebelled when faced with making weapons of war. She then served as a cook in the N.A.A.F.I. – that suited her.

Several of us arranged whist drives and dances. Frank loved whist, he was the best player I ever knew and could wangle an extra trick from even a poor hand. When it was a partner drive, we always played together. He also enjoyed the dances, not because he was a good dancer – his flat uncontrollable feet prevented him from even trying! Instead he played in Combe's dance band (called 'Happy Days') on a drum kit which, with his brother, he had bought before the war. His brother was now in the services so could not join in. Several pianists took turns in playing. The entrance fee was usually sixpence and money raised went for soldiers' benefits – cigarettes were always popular with the troops, so they were bought in thousands. Everyone smoked except me. Combe school was used week after week for these dances. They were our only entertainment.

On the last day of the Christmas holidays, I received an unexpected letter from the education office. Would I report to Long Hanborough infant school instead of Kiddington. Neither the teacher at Kiddington nor at Hanborough knew about my transfer.

29   What a struggle!

During the war every possible effort was made by all, rich or poor, young or old.

As institute members, we were urged to dig up lawns, taught to wash clothes and not iron, to make do and mend, darn and patch, and to save every cabbage leaf and all potato peelings to give to the pigs.

All food was on ration and those institute meetings taught us how to make meals from our gardens, which was just what my mother had been doing all her married life. The only available fruit was home grown.

Even materials, wool, clothes and furniture were on ration. I remember finding skeins of darning wool not on coupon. I immediately bought the quantity allowed and knitted ankle socks to wear over my well-darned stockings.

My mother had always sold eggs, so she had an allocation of stamped eggs to sell on coupon while our eggs were sold to government. The number varied greatly, about one each week in April but maybe only one in two months during the winter. She was allowed a small breakage quota; she valued that extra egg, it would make a lot of potato cakes.

Now I was teaching in Long Hanborough where classes were much larger but happier and I progressed as a consequence. I found teaching Hanborough children very easy. They were level-headed and of similar ability, enthusiastic and eager to learn. These children had only known the war years, they had unexpectedly benefited.

Miss Hayward was head mistress and she understood each child. Some were very poor. We worked together as one and both staff and children enjoyed it.

I must mention that Miss Hayward always allowed Pat Oliver to attend school in her miniature car. Though she was disabled and too old for infant school, we enjoyed her company, it helped her mother and encouraged other children to grow up facing such problems. Thank you Pat, we all remember you.

Miss Hayward left Hanborough and was replaced by Mrs Lawson. At home I became very friendly with Harold and May Adams, whose only daughter, Pam, was the same age as Marion.

Life, I felt, was passing me by, both males and females had one by one left the village. I pondered on the fact that my life was hurrying away from me, as it was from everyone in our age group. Loneliness often directed me to the piano, while Vera Lynn boomed out 'We'll meet again'. My maternal instinct was very strong so I naturally bestowed my love on Marion. I thought I was helping her, she certainly did not lack adult attention. Frank's occupation as baker had kept him from the war and he had flat feet and poor leg muscles after suffering an accident as a four-year-old. He could never have passed an army medical. As life crawled along for the next two years, Frank was nearly the only lad left in the village, likewise I was nearly the only girl. We met more frequently, often cycling miles together. We were now openly courting, it was a comfortable, sympathetic mutual understanding that soothed and shared the stress of both war and loneliness. On my birthday in 1944 we became engaged.

Frank spent six evenings each week making dough, then, getting up early next morning he made the bread, proved and baked it, then he delivered it in a float with 'Old Charlie' to pull it along. The owner of the business seldom came except once a week to pay him £2.10.0. He worked about sixty hours for that. When 'Old Charlie' died a small car was bought to deliver the bread. Frank had no driving lessons and took no test, he just sat in the driver's seat and hoped for the best.

At school Mrs. Lawson kept advising me to get married. Her brother, 'Peter Wilson', was attached to a bomber squadron; life for him was unpredictable. Her schoolmaster husband had just lost his hearing and she was devastated. Her advice was, 'Grab what you can, as early as you can'.

I seldom saw Rose now, since she was working as cook at Combe House, which was used as a rest home for ENSA (Entertainments National Service Association). The ministry of defence was still at Blenheim. At times the village was surrounded by servicemen, usually Americans stationed at Eynsham Hall. Sometimes they were all white and sometimes all black. The farm at Starvell had changed its use to an aerodrome. It was equipped with a decontamination unit just in case the need arose. Aircraft were hidden away in the woods. The lads from the airfield often attended our dances, indeed one of them was a superb pianist and often took a turn on our piano.

My own piano playing was merely plodding along. I played nursery rhymes at school and a few hymns but I did excel on one sixpenny music sheet, 'You Are my Sunshine'.

Winston Churchill was the mainspring behind the allied effort. We knew him as he was born at Blenheim and often attended organised shoots. When in need of a rest he retreated to Ditchley Park.

The government had now introduced double summer time, which meant that when I left home the clock said just after 8 o'clock, but the sun said just after 6 o'clock. This ensured that harvest work could continue till eleven o'clock in the evening.

30   A new life

The war dragged on. The North African coast was captured by the desert rats. Then came the Italian invasion. Activity around us was building up.

Rose was now engaged, but her boyfriend was awaiting with anticipation the invasion of Western Europe as were many thousands. We now had a radio which churned out the news all day every day. On Sundays the service came from St Martin in the Fields. Following the news we endured the national anthems of all the allied nations. I recall being alone at home one day and just to relieve monotony I had dance music on – Joe Loss I think. Dad came in and was appalled – he didn't buy a radio for that rubbish. I turned off the radio and was then accused of being unpatriotic. It was news! news! news!

Music was now leaning towards Glen Miller or the voice of Vera Lynn. Our dances now included The Palais Glide and the Lambeth Walk. 'In the Mood' and jiving was popular. The school where we had the dances was filled with our American friends, and discarded items we had never before heard of were found in the playground next day.

The whole nation was weary and bored as this humdrum life dragged on and on. Would it never end? Frank and I were getting impatient; we walked miles, using up time that could or should have been better spent. We often walked down past the limekiln and round the meadows by the weir. We might spot a kingfisher or a snipe and we always heard curlews. I recall seeing nine noisy stoats following each other over a fisherman's bridge, passing us without even seeing us. I still know nothing about the behaviour of those stoats.

The war speeded along and the cold, sterile atmosphere was changing to a hopeful, optimistic one.

When D-day came it was a massive relief to all. Suddenly thousands of troops left the area overnight. Radios were kept on now. Sadly Rose's boyfriend went missing, believed killed. It was the second tragedy of this sort in her life, so she vowed never to be involved with another man.

Once the war was over, there were celebrations and bunting everywhere, lights came on and signposts reappeared.

My mother was still offering me words of wisdom in her shrewd, crafty ways. She would say to a neighbour, 'I've always told my girls never to consider a boy who does not respect his mother.' Sometimes she would say, 'Don't look at a lad who wears greasy hair and Oxford bags. Make sure you see him in his working clothes.' We talked incessantly about our approach to married life. I had in my short life seen both large families and only children, I had met with both rich children and the very poor. I thought I knew more about the rearing of children than most. I had spent all my days with children, and this was now reinforced by my relationship with Marion.

One day, perhaps quite soon, that point would be tested.

We decided on a family of four, a definite decision never to be questioned. We would have two as close together as possible, a gap of four or five years, then two more. This way no babies would have either too much or too little attention. Our religion, our families, and our education dictated that we had first a house, then a wedding and finally a family, always in that order.

At last we would now be house hunting. During the war I had saved every possible penny, as there was very little to spend it on. One house did come onto the market priced at £1000. We viewed it, but reluctantly agreed that it would not afford the ideal place for children.

Hearing of our plight, Mrs Micklethwaite. who rented a large house, offered us a small secluded cottage in the grounds. Her own contract determined that she could not charge a rent so two hours of gardening by one or other of us was the nominal rent. No rent to pay; a cottage shut off from the road; Yes! Yes!

December 1, 1945.

Yes! We couldn't believe our luck. So suddenly we had a house; even if it was one up and one down, they were quite large rooms.

This was the third time in my life that I would be facing the world in a white outfit. The first was as May Queen in my last year at junior school. My mother could not afford a white dress so my aunt borrowed one from the family where she was in domestic service. The second time was my confirmation in Christ Church cathedral on March 17 1934. The schoolteacher gave us dresses and veils. I think she had them made, but they were handed back to her.

Now, the third time I needed a white dress, Mrs Lawson insisted that I borrowed that of her sister-in-law who had recently married her brother, Peter.

The wedding went forward rather hurriedly to make sure we had the house. The ceremony took place in Combe church on December 1, a warm sunny day. The family rallied with food coupons.

We managed to locate a few bits of secondhand furniture. I had already made some rugs. A cooker could not be found, so in the meantime we just had a primus stove. There were no washing facilities at the cottage so Mum did my white washing and I washed all colours on Saturdays.

We did manage a short honeymoon at the home of Harold's relatives in Cannock. At least we were on our own for one week.

I now recount an incident never previously told. Our honeymoon journey started with a local taxi to take us to Oxford station. After leaving the taxi we crossed over the road, whereupon my suitcase flew open and scattered all my smalls on the road. We glanced back quickly but the taxi had gone so friends and family would never hear of it.

Frank was feeling awful, we had very little drink at the reception but one relative had luckily obtained a few bottles of orange cocktail. It had upset his tummy, so he spent the journey orbiting the corridor of the train. We decided to keep the incident a secret. He felt better the next day.

We agreed that I should continue teaching, but we knew that at some time we would have to manage on Frank's wages, so all my wages were now banked. By February we knew that a baby was on the way. My mother was disgusted. 'It looks as if you couldn't wait,' she said.

'That's the truth,' I retorted.

I was now twenty-five and Frank thirty-five. From now on my focus would be on family, not career.

31   Routine

Now we were anticipating our first-born. Rations were still very meagre but expectant mums were allowed extra milk. As soon as extra milk coupons were offered to the milkman, the news jumped the starting blocks and accelerated around the village. We were offered goat's milk by the local gamekeeper and considered ourselves very lucky

We shared the role of gardening in lieu of rent. Trying to secure a pram was very difficult. I tried several shops unsuccessfully.

Suddenly the keeper's wife said she had a new pram – a Silver Cross. After several unsuccessful attempts to produce a family, they had now given up hope. She needed to be rid of the pram so she offered it to me for the exact price she paid for it before the war – namely £6. What luck!

I carried on teaching until the end of April which gave me a few months to knit and sew; it was smocked dresses and matinée coats and terry towelling nappies in those days.

I attended the Radcliffe maternity unit and was told to expect my baby on September 15. I found pregnancy quite plain sailing – I enjoyed it. Late in pregnancy the baby took up a breach position and had to be turned. First signs of birth came at 1am on September 8. Jim, my brother, was called to bring his car. Frank was sent straight home and told to phone in the morning. Godfrey, my first son, was born at 8 am but he had reverted to a breach position.

That pain was completely forgotten in minutes. I'll never forget that moment, that joy and happiness. Frank was not allowed in until visiting time and other visitors were banned. I just had to lie on my own listening to St. Giles Fair trundling into Oxford as it was St. Giles Sunday morning.

I had very strict ideas about breast-feeding, a rigid routine, every four hours and never fed at night and definitely no dummy.

I think for a baby to be born is truly a miracle but added to this is how milk is induced just when needed. How easy to feed; milk is produced at the correct time, at the correct temperature, never any germs and it gives the baby an inbuilt protection. Just wonderful!! Give him the best, he deserves it, and never will you have cause to feel guilty.

As a child, I remember mothers with plenty of milk helping those less well endowed. This often happened when mums were weaning their babies. Milk will continue as long as baby suckles. Living in a village meant that all details of each parishioner were widely known – it is often called gossip but can be very beneficial.

I proved to be a good milker. The routine was started in hospital as I was there for ten days. Arriving home, we decided that our day would start at five o'clock as that coincided with Frank going to work.

Godfrey was the perfect baby; I would say that, every Mum does. He did not wake in the night. Friends said that I was lucky but routine I'm sure played a part.

First feed 5 am. I got up; then had breakfast – then washed nappies.

Prepared bath for 9 am; next feed, then into the pram in the garden till 1 pm. Next feed, then always went for a walk or visited or shopped.

His next feed was at five; he was laid on a blanket on the floor while we ate our tea. Then into the carry cot and upstairs to bed. I always had to wake him at nine for his last feed.

I did not hurry his feeds, I lingered over him talking and encouraging his coos and smiles.

At five months we already noticed his desire for music, especially classical music. 'You've got a musician,' said my friends but I secretly thought he would be an athlete.

Then came that unforgettable winter when several feet of snow arrived suddenly during the night. The village was cut off from the outside world. Even the main roads were impassable, meaning that a small village must depend on its own manpower. Frank was the only man left at work; his work was essential, he even delivered bread on a sledge. I could not push a pram down the road for about six weeks, but the men had made lay-bys in the snow for overtaking.

The local baker had decided to sell his business. Frank was reluctant to take it on as sliced bread was beginning to arrive. He had worked there since he left school at 14 some twenty-two years earlier. He now went to work for the Hanborough bakery, which was large enough to employ several bakers and complied with regulations on hours of work and holidays. From his previous employer Frank had only had one week's holiday – for our honeymoon – and even then he worked early so he could bake and deliver bread before the wedding.

The occupants of the big house had changed but the 'ground rent' had remained. This couple were trying to start a business so the garden was now a boarding kennels. Mr and Mrs Cresswell had rented a house in Salcombe for a holiday. 'Plenty of room,' they said. 'You can come for a week.'

We travelled down in the dickey seat[16] of their old car. We chugged and rattled along. I had Godfrey on my lap and was six months pregnant. We arrived back home on his first birthday. Godfrey had taken his first steps in Salcombe.

Godfrey was easy to potty train both by day and night. At one year old all nappies were in store ready for the next. There were no extra items to purchase for the next baby, no pram to buy, no carrycot, no clothes or nappies.

My next baby would be born at home, the hospital was only used for first babies. Arrival date was Boxing Day. The district nurse attended a perfect natural birth just four days early. I had pre-named my first daughter Madge, which was actually my mother's choice. She was the most expensive baby I had, as we had to pay the district nurse for all her visits, and because she called in the doctor we had that bill as well. This was the last year with no N.H.S.

We were content. I enjoyed all aspects of my family life. Frank still played his cricket in the summer. I stayed at home when the babies were in bed. We had supreme happiness with our 'pigeon pair'. I often did our gardening rent after they were in bed.

32   In search of a plot

I must relate one story about Frank's time in Hanborough. He always took a sandwich lunch which I prepared each evening. He usually had cheese or spam but always two Marmite sandwiches. He liked his Marmite.

One day on returning he said, 'You forgot my Marmite sandwiches.' I couldn't believe that I had but I apologised, making doubly sure I didn't make the same mistake again.

On arriving home the following day he said the same thing. I knew I hadn't forgotten them. The following day, he verified the fact that a small parcel of Marmite sandwiches was included. At lunchtime they had gone. It took many days to solve the riddle. Kate was a fifteen-year-old who helped at the bakery and although the men did not know it, I guessed she was expecting a baby. She had a craving for Marmite. They did not challenge her. I just put two extra sandwiches in his bag, labelled 'for Kate'. This carried on until she left to have her baby.

At home things started to go wrong. The occupants of the big house had changed again: it was now rented by Mr and Mrs Olive who were probably about sixty years old and would carry on the boarding kennels. But Mrs Olive had two Alsatians that she allowed to run loose in the grounds. No longer could the children play in the garden.

The house now completed on virgin land. Can you spot Frank coming down the drive on his bike? I think those planks of wood made the shuttering used to make the drive.

This was 1948, and the first few private planning applications since the war were being considered. If we could find a piece of ground, maybe we could build. Mr Olive loved his whisky and at every opportunity he would dash down to the local and back again before his wife knew. If she guessed he had gone she would put a padlock on the gate and he was forced to jump over. He often called at our cottage for bicarbonate of soda, and sometimes he would pick my parsley from the garden. The more she tried to stop him, the more he drank every day. Frank's mother lived nearly next door to us and Godfrey often went there but now, when he came back, he sometimes found the gate locked. He was rightly terrified of those two dogs and has remembered this treatment all his life.

Nationally money was very short. Council houses were being built, and six were allocated to Combe. The council had bought one acre for these houses and had arranged for another acre at a future date. This would leave a small plot between the council houses and the wood. The farmer was rightly furious, a small plot of land beneath a row of tall elm trees was no use to him, so we grabbed it.

The estate agent was very unreliable. He used a bicycle as petrol was still rationed. Twice he said he would come to measure the ground but failed to arrive. The third time he arrived in suede shoes to measure a recently ploughed field. He gave a local lad sixpence to go out into the field and hammer in the white peg. The land was never measured – we didn't measure it either – and we had no idea whether it was correct or not. When the council built there some four years later, they said we were about six feet short. This piece of land cost £70.

This would take all of Frank's wages for 14 weeks. There was an imposed limit of £1500 on the house. This would be the amount he could earn in six years. It took several attempts to get the plans passed, as we wanted our house to face south and the council preferred it to face the road. I've always been pleased we won.

My father was retiring so he offered to lend us £600 which was the amount that we could not produce. A mortgage was not considered, I was ignorant of such things. I thought if you bought something you must be able to pay for it. Combe was in the Witney district at the time and they imposed ceilings eight feet six inches high which gives a illusion of a large house when really it is not.

In February 1949 we received planning permission and the house was started in May. One of the hottest driest summers on record, not one spot of rain fell on the building until the roof was on. We were watching the house grow each day, everything falling into place, then oh dear! I realised I was expecting another baby.

Did I sleep *very* soundly one night?

We had planned a gap of four or five years but I was sure I could easily manage. This meant that the fourth baby must quickly follow the third.

In September and October it rained continually and when we moved in at the end of October the ground was covered with ruts made by the vehicles and they were filled with water. We couldn't use the pram until my Dad and brother had made the concrete drive. Village news spread around saying we were having a car, for why else would we have a drive? It was actually made to give the children a space for skates and trikes, scooters and bikes. They loved it; they also had a sandpit.

Godfrey was just three years old and walked and talked so well I even sent him on errands. Cars were still very scarce in the village and there was no anxiety about strangers. He could walk in the road and was encouraged to speak to everyone. One day he went missing. I wasn't very worried, but he knew I liked to know where he was. He returned about an hour later, I could see him coming across the fields. When I asked where he had been, he said, 'I've been to find yonder.' 'Did you find it?' I asked. 'No, it wasn't there.'

He had a very determined, inquisitive mind.

33   Just one hiccough

When moving into our permanent home we had very little money to spend on furniture. We had red quarry tiles in the kitchen and white quarry tiles in the dining room. I had made several rugs from thrums[3] that Mum had managed to get from the wool factory where she obtained the wool for her socks. We had no carpets on the floors or staircase.

I had purchased my first washing machine, a small Hoover, with a mangle that turned inside when packed away. It cost £28 but that was much cheaper than a built-in copper, which most people used at that time.

Our lounge was left empty apart from children's toys, a rocking horse and a doll's pram. The children each had a desk and chair so they could draw or paint. There were hammer pegs, a post box and simple jigsaws so the room was in use when the weather was too wet or severe. In my opinion it was an idyllic position to bring up children. They could be both active and observant yet mostly they were unattended. Our house lies to the south-west of the wood so we are protected from both north and east winds.

We had no car or television so no activities were laid on for them. My own time was spent in the kitchen or the garden. Their diet was rigidly planned. They had some form of protein at every meal. I still went to the health centre at Hanborough each month, where I obtained their ration of orange juice and cod liver oil plus a few extras. These products were not yet on open sale. All my children were good eaters, and I didn't offer them the dreaded porridge.

I recall a visiting speaker at W.I. giving a demonstration on filleting herrings. I found them a cheap, very beneficial food. There were no fast foods, and we were some distance away both from shops and temptations.

My next baby was due on March 1, so if a boy it would be David. We pushed the toys to one end of the lounge and brought our bed down. I had decided to have my baby there to eliminate the stairs for the sake of my mother. By the middle of February we had a heat wave, then on the 27th of February my second daughter, Bridget, was born, another strong, healthy baby – and the other two were pleased. The nurse called it a facial presentation but the baby was perfect.

She was the most contented baby I had. I always had to wake her for feeds. The weather was so kind while Mum was looking after me that the nappies were only on the line a few minutes.

It was at this time that I started to teach the others to read. We read each packet at the breakfast table, and I changed packets each week to ring the changes. They began to take items from the shopping bag just to show me they could read. They could even read a newspaper before they were old enough to go to school. They were not clever or indeed stupid but they benefited from a full-time mother-cum-teacher. Every question asked – and indeed there were many – was answered to the best of my ability.

We needed to pay back my father, but how could I earn some money? The garden was the only asset. We had a large hen run put up under the elms to produce eggs, far more than the family would need. We installed an automatic light for the hens which came on at 2 a.m. This gave them more daylight hours and their laying ability doubled.

A pigsty was built, into which we put a litter of pigs. We accepted any swill that was offered, and by stirring in barley meal we had enough to feed them.

We extended our miniature farm each year: a second pigsty, then a large shed to fatten turkeys for Christmas, and plenty of cockerels. Many neighbours joined my Christmas club so I knew just what was ordered and they knew that it was already paid for. Within the first year I had paid back that £600. Money could now be spent on the family or the house.

By the summer of 1951 I knew my fourth baby was coming, so we decided against a holiday. We had not taken them away yet. In July I had a miscarriage, something I had not experienced before. It was not pleasant and it took some time to recover. Plans were altered and we decided to go to Bournemouth for a week at the end of August. I had bought a twin pushchair that I found very handy. It rained each day in Bournemouth, we hardly had a fine hour, so the children didn't paddle or make sandcastles. Madge decided to fall in one day, fully clothed, even to a gabardine. It was really no holiday but we returned still determined to add one more to our family.

'Wait six months,' the doctor had said, so we were anticipating Christmas.

34   Facing reality

Christmas came and we still shared the same determination, so we approached 1952 very optimistic. We were not disappointed. Bridget was now two years old, but another baby was on the way.

I often walked to the cricket field on Saturdays as Frank was still playing, though this summer he had had a few bouts of lumbago which made playing nearly impossible. When we arrived home one day he said bluntly, 'I'm not going to play again.' He had turned to retrieve the ball and a piercing pain went through his hip. Frank, now forty-two, had enjoyed his cricket but the war years had intervened.

That was a difficult summer for me, as the pregnancy was not proving quite as easy as the others. My baby was expected on September 15, but like the rest, he arrived early on the twelfth.

A beautiful baby boy, so like my first born, and we were all very pleased. He was born in that same room. The midwife was concerned, which puzzled me, as the baby was perfect in my eyes. She just commented that there was far too much water with the birth. I didn't believe her, I didn't *want* to believe her.

I had a nasty attack of indigestion that day, so I called in the doctor. The nurse arrived in minutes, sensing there was something dreadfully wrong with me. She correctly diagnosed an ulcer, thinking I was worried about the baby. I was, in fact, very worried about Frank's hip, which was getting worse.

A few days later the nurse took my baby for a hospital check. I was still in bed. When she arrived home she confirmed that something was wrong, and he would need an operation. I was still not convinced. I went into the Churchill hospital with him, knowing in my heart that we would soon be home again and the baby would be healthy.

There were three mothers in the same position, but the other two babies had deformities so I thought they were much worse off than me. As the babies came back from theatre I was elated, he looked so much better. I know now that he had had a transfusion. I rang home immediately with the news. How ignorant I was!

The surgeon called the mums in one by one. The other two were told that there was nothing medically amiss with their babies.

I was told bluntly that my baby had no gall bladder, and that he could not live more than a few months. I was told to go home and forget him, and they would look after him until the end.

'I certainly will not leave him when he needs me. I shall take him home and care for him till the end,' was my answer. That was just what happened. Frank came to see me that evening and found me pacing up and down under that yellow street lighting.

I brought baby home and kept up breast-feeding. For the next few weeks, Frank and I talked and talked. The baby was christened 'Alec' at home and I kept him in that same room.

Breast-feeding a dying baby is the most heart-breaking experience I've ever had. I had no visitors, I just sat alone in that same room like a martyr; after each feed I had three healthy children to focus on.

Wait two years before thinking about another, was the doctor's advice.

Forget about a fourth baby, was the advice given by several friends.

Frank and I thought seriously about adopting, which was an easy alternative in those days. I rang the agency and they just noted our names and address. 'Ring us again when your baby dies,' they suggested.

He died on December 13. We were already preparing for Christmas in one room while our baby lay still in the other. On that Saturday morning I went upstairs to tell the children. One little daughter just stood and looked, one burst out crying, but Godfrey, now just six, put his arm around me and said, 'I'll look after you Mum.'

I can't explain how I felt, only those who have faced it know. The nurse came in with tablets to dry up my milk supply, but I refused them. Alec was buried on Monday and I was furiously pumping off my milk, then sending it by the bus driver to the premature baby unit at the Radcliffe. It was collected twice daily.

After the funeral, on the Monday afternoon, I rang about adoption. 'Yes,' they promised, 'We have three baby boys at the moment. You can choose which one you like.' 'I'm not going to shop,' I retorted, 'I just want a healthy baby. Which one is the nearest?' He was at the Churchill hospital. The nurse went with me to collect him, accompanied by Bridget, as she was not old enough for school. I breast-fed him in hospital before returning home.

The past few weeks must now be put behind us. Forgotten they could never be, but now I owed my love and attention to the other three.

They had always had a Christmas party so there must be one this year.

Most of the time our new baby, Colin, was kept in that same room; firstly to aid his sleeping and to avoid him taking the limelight. The family must get back to normality as soon as possible.

It was 1952 but most foods were still on ration, so I was handed his ration book which contained his original name and address.

The decision to adopt was made by Frank and myself, we had not discussed it with anyone else, so there was an element of surprise. Clearly some villagers were shocked. The comment of a previous friend was, 'I thought you had enough on your plate.' A friendly old lady looked in the pram and blurted out, 'The old bitch.' She meant, of course, Colin's mother for allowing him to be adopted.

I can honestly say that Colin fitted into the family perfectly and to my knowledge there has never ever been any friction between any of them.

The actual adoption came several weeks later. I asked, 'If in the future Colin wanted to marry one of my daughters, could he?' The answer was 'No.' If he met and wanted to marry one of his sisters he had left behind, could he do so? The answer was 'Yes.' This is far more likely to happen now than winning the lottery!

During the next few years we often had whist evenings in the same room. The families made three or four tables. Rose, who never played whist, would always organise the refreshments.

35   A family united

A few months after our very sad event I was to learn that Frank's youngest sister (another Dorothy) was expecting her first baby. The two of us decided that my multi-purpose room was the ideal place. Those same walls that watched over the departure of one life smiled and welcomed another one into the family.

We were happily settled, an adequate house, an ideal situation, and a beautiful village with nature all around us. One by one the children started school. Frank's hip was gradually deteriorating. He was now working for Jim, my brother, who, like his father, could not make a decent living from the farm. He had turned to poultry. He erected deep litter houses containing thousands of hens. Frank, who was used to delivering bread, now took on eggs and oven-ready roasters. His round was in north Oxford.

Our family complete, we thought of holidays. We would choose the sea for the children's sake but both Frank and I were keen on seeing picturesque parts of the country as yet unknown to us.

A chalet for six was advertised in Borth, facing the sea. This proved ideal. I knew that I would cater, but I was prepared. There was no way we could take four small children into any other type of accommodation.

Jim said, 'Borrow my vehicle,' it was an Austin countryman. This was the most economical holiday, I suggested Frank's elderly mother and autistic sister should come with us. Like us they had not had a holiday before. How we all got into that vehicle – carrycot included – I'll never know, but we did and we all enjoyed it.

The chalet was perfect, we visited a different spot each day, travelled on a welsh miniature railway, it was grand.

I never regretted taking my in-laws, they talked incessantly about it, but neither lived for many years afterwards. I felt that we had repaid some of the help that many other relatives and friends had so recently given us.

The following few years we rented caravans in different sites, usually rented a car, as Frank was still able to drive. We enjoyed those years; catering was easy, we took vegetables from our garden and a square cake.[7] It was a carefree week for the children.

My old piano was transferred to our home and as each child reached the age of eight they took piano lessons with a local teacher.

At the age of ten Godfrey joined the scouts in Stonesfield, this meant cycling but he needed social activity, this involved camping.

All this time Frank was becoming less mobile, the pain in his hip was unbearable. The doctor sent him to Mr. Scott at the Wingfield hospital (now the Nuffield). He was pioneering hip operations. This operation was explained to Frank. His femur would be broken and re-aligned. I visited him daily which meant family and friends would supervise at home. We had no car so I travelled by evening train, then bus up to the hospital. Our children were for - one year only – all attending the primary school. We had just purchased a television so 'Andy Pandy' would help to amuse them.

Mr Scott called it a successful operation but Frank's leg was now splayed outward so he could never ride a bicycle again.

He was at home for ten months, most of that time on crutches – his hip joint was supposed to be rid of pain. He tried to return to egg delivery and although I accompanied him for several months it did not really work out and he was obliged to leave his job.

This was putting far more responsibility on me, in truth we had more money from the garden than from his work. We had erected a garage to store animal foods, we borrowed many broody hens[13] from Jim, and I was hatching chicks, ducklings or goslings. We had a large shed for turkeys. I ran a Christmas club for the neighbours.

Frank could not dig now so we were desperate to find a job that he could do.

Band members:
Frank Calcutt, Roger Evins, Godfrey Calcutt, Violet Nunn, Susan Barrett, Madge Calcutt, John Nunn (Jun)
Richard Everitt, Ron Oliver, Geoffrey Barrett, Jill Oliver, Angela Nunn, Sandra Bright, Dorothy Calcutt, Stan Soame, Bernard Barrett
Norman Barrett, Stephen Abbott, John Evins, Bridget Calcutt, Graham Soame, John Nunn (Bandmaster) Linda Soame, Jenny Waistie, Norma Franklin, Kathleen Barrett, Patricia Nunn

City Motors at the Wolvercote roundabout were advertising for a forecourt attendant. We travelled together by bus to go to the interview. Frank was despondent as the job involved shift work, meaning the hours were not consistent with bus timetables. But as he could still drive, and although he was reluctant, I pressured the firm to provide a car that adapted to a family of six. 'We've got a Vauxhall Wyvern in today. It will cost you £535.'

We had £500 in the bank plus a few more pounds at home, so the following week we were a happy family – but on the rocks again.

Frank was a renewed man. His work proved successful, he received tips at work and had the satisfaction of contributing once more to the family purse. The car, with a bench seat in front, could hold us all. I started driving lessons immediately.

Godfrey passed his examination and started at Chipping Norton Grammar School. Combe had no bus service so a bike ride to Stonesfield each day was necessary. His piano lessons were transferred to Mrs Wheeler in Woodstock, and a permit to cycle across the park was granted.

After returning from scout camp he begged for a brass instrument. One scout, a member of Stonesfield brass band, had a cornet and played 'Reveille' and 'Cook house door'. Godfrey borrowed it, found it easy and was determined by hook or by crook to get an instrument. Getting lessons in Combe was impos-

All at Combe Primary School: Colin, Godfrey, Madge and Bridget.

sible, so in desperation I said, 'Bike over to Stonesfield, find the bandmaster, and listen to him.'

He was gone, and came home again with an old baritone4 strapped to his back. That instrument was never idle that week. Both Madge and Bridget could play it. Their piano lessons had helped them. Colin was not encouraged until his adult front teeth had grown.

After much begging I allowed Madge to attend his lesson the following week. There were no more instruments available, so they shared the baritone. Bridget followed the next week, still only nine. The bandmaster's comment was, 'How many more does your Mum have at home?'

As Stonesfield parishioners had collected the money to purchase the instruments, I thought, living in Combe, it was only fair for us to buy our own. I approached Mr Nunn – the bandmaster – and he ordered secondhand instruments – a baritone for Godfrey, a trombone for Madge and a cornet for Bridget. As far as I remember they cost £14 each.

The trombone was a few days later arriving so Godfrey cycled to Stonesfield to collect it. The rep who sold animal foods called that day and said, 'Do you know where Godfrey is?' 'Yes,' I replied, 'He has gone to collect a trombone for Madge.' 'He is sitting on the rounders5 playing it,' he said.

From that moment on he pleaded for the trombone. The bandmaster did not readily agree but eventually Godfrey and Madge swapped instruments. Bridget was happy with the cornet.

I soon passed my driving test and was able to convey them to band practice.

I sat in the car outside clicking my knitting needles.

Colin joined when he was eight and I was encouraged to play the drums; they could not really be classed as percussion. I was envious of my children and pondered over the possibility of my playing too. After they had gone to school, I ventured upstairs to the boy's bedroom armed with a cornet and a tutor. Playing it gave me a boost and got rid of that deprived feeling I had had since my sister was given piano lessons. I went into the band and Frank played the drums. All of us were now in band uniform. Looking back I think that playing a keyboard is a lonely, solitary occupation, whereas a brass band encourages teamwork, loyalty, community spirit and companionship. We played for religious services, fetes, concerts and contests. It is a rewarding but time-consuming occupation. Listen intently to a committed Salvation Army band, it matters not what they are playing, but heart and soul is poured into that music. Chords, crescendos and diminuendos create that emotion and sentiment. 'Deep Harmony' is rightly named.

Thousands of young people are introduced to music via brass bands but I think they are still scorned and classed as the poor man's music.

We had an old Belgian bugle that Frank's father had picked up at Ypres during the First World War. What a blessing! When my children could not be located, I would play 'Cook house door'. Hungry youngsters would race back home and the rest of the world would know that our meal was ready.

One Sunday afternoon we were playing by the Windrush at Bourton-on-the-Water. A gust of wind whipped off our music and deposited it in the river. Bridget, still in white ankle socks, took them off and paddled to rescue it. It was lucky that the current was quite slow.

36   Career or family! Marrying the two

Easter 1959 brought a visit from Mrs Lawson. I had not seen her since I had left Hanborough. She was now head teacher at Cogges School in Witney and intended retiring at the end of August. She had a vacancy for the seven-to-nine-year-olds and wondered if I would consider helping her for the summer term. She thought the incoming head should fill the post on a permanent basis.

She offered to collect me and bring me home again. I was loathe to do it but in the past she had been extremely kind to me so reluctantly I agreed. I didn't really need the money so my first cheque went straight to ERNIE (Premium Savings Bonds). He has kept it safe for me; I wonder if he knows it is still there.

I'd now got four children to cater for, pigs in the sty, about a hundred hens, turkeys and a large profitable garden. I was taking the family to band practice twice a week. I was still very enthusiastic.

That summer was the first for Godfrey at senior school. I visited their annual sports day. Godfrey was a very athletic lad and appeared keen. I had bought him 'spikes' for running and he had entered the mile. I watched eagerly as did other mums. Godfrey won by half a lap, and I thought such a win boded well for the future. The sports master spoke to me anticipating his prospects.

The autumn term came and Madge joined Godfrey at senior school. Each week I asked him for his sports kit to wash. There was always a qualified reason why it had not been used. I didn't delve any further into the situation.

His report for sports at Christmas stated 'No attendance this term.' An explanation was needed. It turned out that the brass teacher I had badgered for was now giving lessons, and the conflicting timetable meant that Godfrey must choose, music or sports. He wasn't certain of my viewpoint on such a decision that could affect his career so he grabbed music without consulting me.

I had now been back in teaching for one summer term, and the lure of teaching was uppermost in my thoughts. Colin, my youngest, was now eight years old. Could I go back to teaching even if I elected to do it?

After the war years the National Union of Teachers had specified that they would not work with uncertificated colleagues. Ten years of such teaching would automatically qualify any teacher. Less experience meant two years at teacher training college. I had worked for nine and a half years. I rang the local education committee asking if I could go to Westminster College. The same treasurer was still there as when I passed my examination years before.

'You can start teaching immediately,' he said. 'We are desperate for teachers; I accept you. I say you are qualified.' I had returned when teachers were in great demand. So I restarted at Woodstock Primary School. I had always thought that teaching had made me a better parent but now I knew that parenthood had transformed my teaching. The school was next to the garage in Oxford Road, but a very old building. The population of Woodstock was increasing so class numbers were soaring.

Frank was happy in his work but his hip was painful. Among the customers at the petrol station was Mr. Scott, the surgeon. He was assessing Frank's progress and was not satisfied. He explained his new techniques and suggested another operation. The alignment of the leg could never be altered but the ball of the hip joint could be replaced by a metal one.

As I was now involved in teaching, I gradually rid myself of pigs and poultry. Rose lived opposite us with her widowed mother. Each morning when all of us had left for school, Rose's mother would take up ashes, sweep and wash the breakfast dishes. I paid her £1 a week. This was a help to us both. Rose's mother always pulled Madge's leg. A school bus had now been allocated to Combe but when Madge left for the school bus each morning, she would dash to a certain apple tree and grab the largest she could find. Even if the bus had already gone past, she managed to secure an apple. Madge, you will never live down those Charles Ross apples.

Bridget went on to Chipping Norton school and Colin was the only one left at the primary school. He was secretly worried that he wouldn't pass the examination to attend the same school, in which case he would not get the same music teaching. One day he was reading *The British Bandsman* and saw an advertisement for a cornet player in Woomera, Australia. Although only ten, he wrote asking for the post. He received an answer suggesting he carried on with practice and he would be considered when he was older.

The family were bursting with enthusiasm about music. One teacher, very keen on jazz, started a jazz group, which needed different instruments. Godfrey chose tenor saxophone, Madge chose alto saxophone, Bridget (still at primary school) played trumpet and a clarinet alternated between them.

That WI market stall now resided on the pebbles of Woodstock Town Hall. How convenient now I was teaching. Mum got there with her produce just after eight and I needed to be at school just a bit later. She carried on until she was ninety, and it gave her a reason for living.

37   Any spare time?

The animals and poultry now gone, the large slice of land under the elm trees was planted as lawn. I bought a sit-on mower so cutting it was a pleasure and not a chore.

We did not neglect our week-long annual holiday. It was always a caravan holiday and our Wyvern was the means of travel. We always took our square cake[7] with us. In good weather we visited the nation's well known spots. We visited Land's End, the summit of Snowdon, and Blackpool tower ballroom where we listened to Reginald Dixon.

On wet days we searched out factories that allowed visitors – The Coats factory in Preston, the carpet factory in Axminster. Once I remember calling at the Symbol biscuit factory just outside Blackpool. 'We don't usually allow people round but a local school is just starting, you can join them.' I'm sure they thought we were a private school. Everyone enjoyed it – they gave us a light afternoon tea and a packet of chocolate cookies each as we left. Similar trips prevented any moaning in wet weather.

We always looked for notices of where local bands were playing. The children would talk to the players or bandmaster and on invitation would chase back to the car for their own instrument. They loved playing with seaside bands, who always have an inbuilt camaraderie.

Back home, Frank's left hip was so painful that Mr Scott suggested a replacement hip which, he assured him, would be perfect.

While Frank's hip was improving Oxford United had been promoted to the football league so together with Colin we went to see their last match before promotion. I think it was against Witney Town, it was a happy, noisy atmosphere; we had all enjoyed village football but now we were hooked on Oxford.

I was using up every minute of my time; I had started teaching Robin to play the cornet in the dinner hour at school but many others wanted to join. I had recently bought all my children new instruments so I lent out their old ones.

We bought a Renault 8, with an automatic gear change which was more convenient for Frank. I bought a minibus for £195 to use both for family and the band members and the poor old Wyvern that now had 165,000 miles on the clock would be used by Godfrey. This year all four children were at grammar school, Godfrey was a prefect and seemed to attract the girls. He had decided to make a career in music. We tried in vain to talk him out of it. For the last two years he had been playing in the English Schools' Orchestra, which involved a music course during the Easter holidays. Once again more girls were attracted, I couldn't even keep up with all the names.

Early that spring he had an interview at the Royal Northern College of Music. At the interview he was told he had been accepted, I think he already had music at A level standard. Whatever results he had he knew he would be heading for Manchester in September.

I was back in teaching and enjoying every minute. Had I really been away from it for fourteen years? This was where I belonged and I was both wanted and welcomed. I didn't exactly get any spare time.

Through carolling efforts at Christmas the band had more instruments, and children came from many villages. There were so many at Woodstock that we used one afternoon for a brass band. A primary school with its own brass band! I owe a big 'thank you' to the headmaster who took responsibility for my class.

I was often asked if I was wasting my time, as so many would fall by the wayside. I don't think that is the point, as any introduction to music is better than none. I have had reports from all over the country of pupils who started their music career at Woodstock Primary School.

When Stonesfield band was contesting, we often met players from other bands whose families had moved on from Woodstock and they had joined their local band. I emphasise again that brass playing can be enjoyed by all. I have never seen such a cocktail of human beings – rich and poor, old and young, strong and weak – drawn together wearing identical uniforms to play one specific piece of music. At a contest you can hear that nominated piece of music twenty or thirty times and never get tired of it. It is an all-embracing hobby down a straight road but it has so many side turnings. Playing a brass instrument has also often been used as therapy to fight against asthma.

The brass band world is divided into sections, very similar to the football league. We were then in the fourth section as we had just started and most of the members were beginners. Under the baton of John Nunn, the Stonesfield band was promoted and now, some forty years later, currently under the baton of Terry Brotherhood, they are up near the top. They even played in a contest in the Albert Hall. There are still about ten players who started with me. Robin, my first beginner at Woodstock, is a very valued cornet player.

Best of banding to you for the future!

How Godfrey managed to trick his way into the Oxford Territorial Army band, I do not know, but he did and one evening each week he bussed straight to Oxford. This was a military band, not brass alone. I recall one night I went as usual to meet him at the Combe turn where he got off Worth's bus. We had an agreement that if he could not catch the bus, I would go to Oxford and pick him up in Beaumont Street. One night he did not get off the bus so I carried on into Oxford to find him – it was about 11 pm. I returned home without him only to find he had dozed off in the coach and had a long walk home from the next stop.

At about this time my older sister married. In the evening she had engaged a band for a dance. The kids grabbed their instruments and played with the group. Bridget now had a trumpet so it blended well and she even played a solo part. They were invited to join the Mick Muller band in Cowley where they had dances on Saturday evenings.

My school group was improving enough to join the inter-schools brass band. This entailed a massed band in Birmingham Town Hall. All bands had practised set pieces and now they were playing with hundreds of others. Twice a child from my party was chosen to play a solo, and both did well. Thank you to Andrew Kinch and Nicky Merry.

Nicky Merry had started his school life in my class, asked for an instrument, and did so well his father bought him his own. He was also good at football and idolised George Best. He was later chosen for the national schools football team and played many times. He joined Oxford United but injury took him out of the game after a few years.

I had introduced several girls to my group and there were many raised eyebrows. Brass bands with girls in a town like Woodstock! It was surprising how many parents were longing to join in – and they did. Among those still playing are Phil Hoare, Carlo Bonasera, Paul Spencer, Val Reade and Harry Goldstein. These were all parents who joined because their offspring had unintentionally motivated them.

Frank was now much happier, the operation was more successful – but the right hip was now becoming painful.

38   Busy people

In 1969 a course for brass teachers at Durham was advertised in the local education paper. It would take place in the first week of holidays. It was financed by the Oxford Education Committee and I relished it. This was a chance to enjoy playing with no responsibilities. This was the best holiday for me – no catering – new friends to converse with. We stayed at St. Chad's college and played in the cathedral meeting room. I came home with a cassette of our efforts during the week and made friends and family envious. I was now convinced that brass groups should be given collective training, which was taboo with Oxford Education Committee.

I remember the day Colin came home from school and asked, 'Mum, what is a navvy?' Quite innocently I replied, 'Someone who works very hard but rarely gets anywhere.' 'Well,' he said, 'the brass teacher called me a brass band navvy today.' That same teacher brought a brass quartet to perform at our school. At question time, one lad who was already playing a cornet with me asked, 'What is the difference between a cornet and a trumpet?' The answer was, 'A trumpet is a man's instrument.' I had to sit and endure such a bigoted answer. There were two sisters listening whose father was a superb cornet player in the Salvation Army. I was called to the music department of the education committee and told that, as Godfrey was playing in the English Schools Orchestra, he would have to leave the local band. He could not possibly play in both treble and bass clef. I thought for a few seconds then replied, 'If that band had not welcomed and taught him none of my family would now be involved in loving and living music. He is already playing in two clefs; that's how it stays.'

In the early sixties when I was secretary of the Stonesfield band we organised solo contests for juniors. There was always a huge entry, nearly too many to cope. One small group came from Bedworth in Leicestershire. Leicestershire always had a broader approach to their instrumental teaching. Just like Durham, trumpets and cornets, french horns and tenor horns, basses and tubas all played together and any clef was used. One particular boy started coming at the age of eight and progressed until fourteen. He never failed to win his age group and at fourteen he won the English junior championship and so qualified to play with the seniors. Yes, he won that as well. He is now the best trumpet and cornet player in the country. You'll often see the name 'James Watson' zooming up your television screen at the end of a programme. He has conducted the Black Dyke Mills Band one of the best-known brass bands.

I retired in 1980, just when a new director of education was appointed. Mr Tim Brighouse took a different view. I still gave my services to a few schools. When I was taking a group at Queen Emma's Dyke School in Witney – thanks to Mr Barry Rogers – he walked in unannounced. He was full of praise. 'This is how I wish it to continue here,' he said. I had made a small contribution towards change.

Apart from hundreds of bands in the country with varying standards many players do prefer orchestras, military bands or pop groups. The standard on football terraces needs to improve, but music is for all.

The trip to Durham was proposed again the following year but so many wanted to join in. Both Madge and Bridget went, as did Bridget's boyfriend, although she was only sixteen (this trombone player became her husband a few years later). While we were there Madge met a French horn player and they also married a year later.

Godfrey, who always found a holiday job, had joined Billy Smart's circus for the summer while it was touring Scotland. He was of course in the band that was shattering the silence at the start of each performance with the sounds of 'The Sabre Dance'.

Frank was recovering from the operation on his right hip and hoping it would be the last. Both the small Renault and the minibus were proving to be good buys. I was still keeping the whole of the garden productive. Frank could hoe but not dig, which suited me because I hated hoeing.

In her last year at school Madge had applied to many colleges but, being a girl, she was told in every case to write again when she had her exam results. Madge had always been very artistic but above all she excelled in maths and science. She decided she would study architecture and as soon as her results were known, many colleges were willing to accept her. She went to South London and joined the Crystal Palace brass band. She decided not to finish the course but to turn her attentions to computing. How fruitful it was; she soon ascended the ladder and finished right at the top.

How times change! When she was in London, I would take her to the London Road roundabout and she would hitch hike. It wasn't even considered dangerous.

Bridget's aim was to become a teacher and that never changed. She went to training college in Reading. She left school in 1968 and suddenly Colin said, 'I'm going to go into an army band.' He was not very tall at the age of fifteen, but he was accepted into the Royal Green Jackets. That summer both Bridget and Colin left Chipping Norton School. Colin reported to Winchester, where he met up with another lad who had been playing with a local band. Friends again for army life. Colin suddenly grew and is now as tall as any of the others.

Godfrey had become serious with Pat and would be married in the summer of 1969. Pat had already been dictating to him. 'If you consider a career in playing music, don't count on me. I don't want a life staying at home alone in the evenings, you change your mind to teaching and we will share our lives together.'

The house was sometimes empty now, but often it was overpopulated.

I now had fewer responsibilities, just Frank, teaching, the house and garden, Stonesfield band and trips to Oxford United whenever possible.

Both girls were married in 1971, Bridget in July and Madge in August. They had very different weddings. Bridget had a marquee on the lawn and the Stonesfield band playing, she even played a solo in her wedding dress. Madge had a quiet wedding with the reception in The King's Arms in Woodstock.

Madge's husband was a schoolteacher and french horn player while Bridget's was a dental technician and trombone player.

At this time the Woodstock School was taking groups of children to Yenworthy near Exmoor. I went twice because I could drive a minibus and there were two in use at the hostel. John Brucker, the headmaster, went the first time and we all enjoyed the long walks with sandwich lunches. He, a bird watcher all his life, taught us a lot, but secretly I thought I knew more about trees. It was energetic but it suited me, and those children still remember the trips.

At this time my father's health was deteriorating and he died in April 1971. My mother was alone now, so I must give more time to her. I started taking her on trips, we would go one day, have bed and breakfast then return the following day. Meanwhile Frank and I were finding a lot more time for watching football. We went to several away matches. Oxford were gradually climbing the league. I remember taking the minibus filled with boys, only to find no parking space at the Manor; I dropped off the boys and travelled a very long way to park, returning to find the Manor gate was locked. I appealed to the door keeper explaining the boys were without anyone to take charge. He gave way to me – thank you.

Mr Arthur Turner was the manager at Oxford and I approached him with a view to our band playing at football matches. We played several times both before the match and at half time. We collected money by four of us walking round with a blanket. Can you imagine that today? There was never any trouble, the fans were proud of their aiming skills.

The three married offspring all had mortgages, so because money was short for them, I bought a caravan which Godfrey towed to a site for the season and that suited us all.

Colin celebrated his twenty-first birthday with us all at a hotel in Leicestershire, which was equidistant from our homes. He was then embarking to Germany. It meant he would miss Oxford matches at Christmas but Nigel Cassidy very kindly recorded a Christmas message from Oxford United.

One year the caravan was sited on the north coast of Wales. Frank and I went during the Easter holidays to secure the spot. The welsh owner was very quick to take our money as he was so excited about the Welsh-English rugby match to be played at Cardiff that day. I'm sure we benefited, paying less than we should, anyway he got to the match in plenty of time and Wales won.

1974 brought the first grandchild, a son for Godfrey and Pat. I was at school when the message came, the secretary stayed with my class when I was wanted on the phone. I just ran round the school telling everyone the news, they all thought I was crazy. Perhaps I was, but they hadn't got a grandchild. Babies do something for me.

We decided to go to the caravan for a week with Godfrey and Pat and baby. I arrived with a very stiff neck. The next few days it worsened till Godfrey took me to the local doctor. 'I think you should go straight home,' he said, so Godfrey drove us back that evening. I called in our doctor and he diagnosed pneumonia. When I was better he sent me for a chest X-ray. The results showed a patch on the thymol gland. The gland had to be removed and the surgeon said, 'I advise you to give up smoking.' He clearly did not believe that I had never smoked. Passive smoking had not been heard of then.

Madge advised me to sell the minibus and buy a small car; this was the first of many small Renaults.

39   End of holidays

The school was doing a project on Victorian times. My classroom was changed, it had peg rugs[15] on the floor and trays of sand to write in.

I wrote a play for the children to act. Mrs Sharp, the secretary, printed it out for me. It was really based on my mother's family as she could remember it. John Brucker, the headmaster, invited my mother to talk to the children about the changes in the way of life in Woodstock. The children could not believe that unemployment had always existed. So she told them what her brothers and indeed her husband had done to secure a job.

At this time I spent time with my mother most evenings and I jotted down every detail of what she told me. Both Mr Brucker and Mrs Sharp were urging me to write a book. I thought such history should be recorded – but could I write a book? It had never been even my wildest dream.

The Stonesfield band had difficulty in finding a room for practices. So eventually they bought a large, portable shed and erected it at the end of my garden. It wasn't beautiful, it didn't have all mod cons but the band now had about sixty members and it lent itself to small groups.

Our house being on the south side of a wood is quite a warm spot and flies liked to hibernate in the band room. As soon as the heaters were on, out came the flies and we could do nothing to prevent it. The villagers enjoyed the band being there, and although it is not used now for playing, the room is still being used as a store for their library.

Colin had spent these years travelling with the Green Jackets. He did spells in Germany, Oman, Cyprus, Hong Kong and Northern Ireland. He was demobbed in 1979.

In 1975 Frank retired but he was still having hip trouble. Another operation loomed and this time it proved more permanent. We bought a greenhouse, hoping that Frank would get more out of gardening. Then we enlarged the lounge (that multi-purpose room), fitting large double-glazed south-facing windows.

The following year was very hot and dry. Dutch elm disease spread across the country, and our row of elms was dying. Within twelve months they had all been felled. Something now must be done with that large plot of ground.

One day, during the drought, I came home at lunchtime. Birds were flying everywhere so I knew something was amiss. The birdbath had dried up and they were all very thirsty. As I filled it they came down to drink. One bird was very different, I had never noticed that blue one before. It was a nuthatch. I resolved to come home each day to ensure the birds did not die of thirst. On returning to school I noticed a field covered with lapwings, several of which were the golden variety. I mentioned it to Mr Brucker who went immediately to verify it.

Holidays during this decade were all taken in the caravan but this came to a sudden halt. We had several grandchildren now and Frank reluctantly decided to stay at home. He loved the soaps and reading took a lot of his time. Our own children were looking for holidays beyond these shores and 1980 saw the last caravan holiday in Norfolk.

Godfrey came home with his pigeon pair now aged four and six. I took them to London and we travelled around in an open top bus.

This year saw the end of my teaching career. They were asking teachers to retire – why? why? why? There were plenty of children, but very little money to spend on education. I came back to teaching when there were few teachers available, now they wanted me gone. They offered to make my years up to sixty-five which meant I would get an extra five years' pension. I retired but carried on taking brass classes for several years at Woodstock Primary, Queen Emma's Dyke in Witney, and several villages including Hailey.

My eyes were giving me trouble, I had glaucoma in both of them. I was dropping out of playing because operations were imminent.

Colin had no girl friend but he soon found Linda, a cornet player from our band whose marriage was unsuccessful. She was left with two small children. She is the daughter of John Soame who deals in secondhand goods and antiques. Car boot sales and auctions attract Linda like a magnet.

Another brass player had joined the family. All my four were now brass players and three had married brass players. Pat, who was not a brass player was a pianist, and also has a beautiful voice. Once when the band gave a concert eight of us played a double quartet and Pat wielded the baton. Bridget is following me and now has a junior band in the school at Ambrosden where she teaches.

40   On the Cotswold way

Now Frank and I were at home together, but Frank's age together with his physical disabilities prevented holidays. He was quite content to read and watch soaps but now we had season tickets to the Manor. He had a seat in Beech Road while I still stood on the terraces. Oxford United was making history

I think I have stood in every part of that ground. Managers came and went, players came and went. We clapped and we barracked, we cheered and we jeered. But sadly Oxford was accumulating debt. One hundred and twenty six thousand pounds. Robert Maxwell bailed us out. He was a character, but we must admit he kept Oxford afloat at that time.

While Frank was reading and watching the soaps I sat with a pad on my lap and scribbled away. This was the birth of my first book. I still had no thought about publishing: I just thought that a family with such a background should be catalogued somewhere.

After taking those two grand children to London I suggested I took them for another trip the following year. Now there were four of them old enough to go, but I could still manage four in my car so we went to Portsmouth. We hoped we would see the 'Mary Rose' but she had not yet surfaced, so we went into the museum of artefacts that had already been rescued, then a trip around 'The Victory' before returning home.

This was a black day for The Green Jackets, the occasion of the Regent's Park bombing. Colin was devastated; he showed feelings of sorrow and even guilt. Mates he had known and lived with for so long, now blown out of exis-tence. They had called at Combe several times when on tour, a friendly jovial bunch. I had even gone to London to purchase a specified French horn mouth-piece and sent it to Hong Kong. It was for John McKnight whose local band had rivalled ours years before; John had joined the army on the same day as Colin. Now, sadly, just a headstone and two little girls without a father.

What would I do the next year? Two more would be old enough to come with me so another means of transport must be found. Madge came to the rescue. We would hire a minibus for a few days, she would drive while I sat in the back with the children. She had no family but she loved her nieces and nephews.

These trips – this was the first of many – usually started early on the Wednesday after Easter, returning on the Friday. We had two nights B and B. The trips were very successful. The children loved them. Godfrey's family came from Manchester, Bridget's from Oakley and Colin's from Witney. This was keeping the family as a unit. Each grandchild must be four years old to join, which ensured that they could carry their own suitcase. With so many discipline prevailed and with me in charge the trips were loosely educational.

We stopped for picnic meals, when each child kept to his own task. One put out the chairs, one lit the stove for coffee, one poured out the cold drinks and one put the blanket and cushions for the smallest to sit on. I remember the youngest saying, 'What can I do?' I allowed him to buy sweets in the shop and hand them round in the bus.

Easter proved to be a good time of the year to organise such trips. There is far less traffic than in the summer. It is much easier and cheaper to park. It is easier to enter the worthwhile attractions. And it is very easy to get B and B – we had very little trouble even with so many children.

I wanted to take up walking, so with the help of the *Combe Courier* I found several other enthusiastic hikers. We would walk the Cotswold Way which starts at Chipping Campden and ends at Bath, a distance of just over one hundred miles. My own son Colin was very keen, and many more joined in. At the time Colin was a milkman so he started and finished a day's work very early. We arranged the first walk from the church at Chipping Campden to Broadway. One car was taken to Broadway to enable the other drivers to collect their own cars. This proved a wealth of experience, every bend or twist in the track brought a new aspect. The world took on a leisurely pace. Walkers travelling the opposite way would stop for a chat.

This was a nature, history and geological lesson all in one. We were not alone, some organised parties had a leader and a whipper in. That didn't appeal to me, I wanted to look at each monument, tree or even a long forgotten flower such as a bee orchid or quaker grass. As we descended towards Hailes Abbey that Thomas Cromwell had once set on fire, we passed a lovely fruit farm and were tempted in.

It was like an oasis in a desert, initially just a fruit shop, but local farms have added their wares – jams and chutneys from one, homemade ice cream from another. Anything that can be produced within a thirty-mile radius is there. The farm combines nature walks with pick-your-own, and even caters for your caravan. The entrance is about two miles north of Winchcombe on the same road as Hailes Abbey but quite accessible to coaches. So much homegrown and homemade produce, mature cheese and ham and apple juice, but don't miss their homemade soup in the restaurant.

There were so many historic sites that suddenly met us. There were long barrows including Belas Knap, and we counted the 'Seven Springs'. We saw Coopers Hill where the cheese rolling takes place, and looked round the beautiful church and cemetery at Painswick. There was Cleeve Hill, which the others managed to climb but I needed to go up on all fours – what a sight! We walked through a beech wood, tall and straight, obviously planted too close and the trees had reacted accordingly. They must have produced some beautiful timber. Crab apples and wild pears dotted the fields and plenty of wild strawberries fruited along the lanes. Walking the ridge gave one a sense of well-being, and as we looked down on Cheltenham and Gloucester we were literally on top of the world.

This is the way to see the Cotswolds although it was not always perfect, what with slippy, muddy slops and occasionally a low flying jet. Many joined in the walk but four of us managed the whole distance; Fred Rawlings, Phil Hoare, Colin and myself.

41   Trees

I was now occupied at home. I had, since my childhood days, a passion for trees and now I had a large area to plant. Our soil is alkaline, so acid-loving trees must be avoided. I read many books. Rose and I joined The Friends of Westonbirt and went to their Sunday meetings. I went with Rose to the Hillier arboretum in November just to discover which trees were attracting birds so late in the season. There were trees for windbreaks, trees for beautiful flowers, trees for autumn colour but trees for berries and bird habitat were top of my list.

We already had one tree which we planted as a plum stone when we first bought the ground in 1949. It is a *prunus cerasifera* with very red leaves (often called a cherry plum). It has proved an asset as it attracts bullfinches – beautiful birds but orchard owners would not agree. Bullfinches eat the flower buds in January and February. When our tree blooms in April, it only has blooms on the lower branches. We really planted it for the fruit, but we love the birds and it has deterred the finches from our plum trees.

Our small corner of hazels have proved a blessing for the nuthatches. To appeal to the larger birds such as blackbirds, thrushes, fieldfare and redwing there is no tree as successful as the large cotoneasters. They are beautiful, they have flowers in spring, berries in autumn, and as soon as frost appears the birds swoop down. I think *cornubia* is the best, while *watereri* is a close second.

The decorative crabs will also coax in the larger birds. Jays often feed on ours. I did plant a golden hornet crab but it is useless. The birds would not touch it, the crabs rotted and dried on the tree. That had to go, John Downie is by far the best. *Crataegus prunifolia* has proved equally successful.

I planted a windbreak of conifers to shelter the birds where I hang the peanuts. They also provide a home for spiders and the tits love the spider eggs.

We are lucky to have a very large oak tree in the wood which was struck by lightning a few years back. Dead bark curls around its branches, but all is not lost; I saw a tree creeper feeding its young one day with insects from the bark. I think the curled-up bark had provided a nest for the bird. The oak tree is host to so many caterpillars and loopers, while the acorns also make a meal for many birds and animals.

I looked out of my bedroom window in the early hours one morning and saw a fox eating dried cotoneaster berries. This was in April and the vixen was heavily pregnant. I was sorry for her so I decided to give her a better meal the following night. I always put out one egg now and maybe a handful of peanuts. Hedgehogs and the fox often feed together. We have also seen muntjac, occasionally deer, and one winter we had a regular visit from a badger.

I actually watch the ways of the birds so close to my window. Did you know that spotted woodpeckers grow yellow feathers around their beaks in early spring? I've watched the nuthatch that always feed upside-down. If it gets a small piece of peanut it will swing back its head to swallow it. It prefers an upside-down feeder. I fill the feeder with peanuts, then pour on hot dripping. I bought a nicely thatched bird table, but in the spring the blackbirds claimed the thatch to make their nests. I never feed birds with bread, it only brings in unwanted ones that should be feeding in the fields. Starlings don't need bread, let them eat the creepy crawlies in the open ground. My garden is littered with bird boxes and feeders, positioned to be viewed from at least one window. One spring we actually had a nightingale, it was singing at midnight and again during the next morning, but alas no more.

We've always had plenty of woodpeckers, green ones on the lawn eating ants and leather jackets, masses of greater spotted on the nut feeders – but this year lesser spotteds have been coming in regularly. I wonder why they have suddenly appeared? When we first came here we saw plenty of partridges, sadly no more, but we still see and hear a few skylarks in the spring. For several years we did not see a thrush, but we have a pair here again now. We used to have a spotted flycatcher nest each year but not any more. We once had a pied flycatcher but it only stayed one night. It must have been migrating.

Rose has retired now so we often go out together. When we were in Devon, we once left the car in Lynmouth and walked to Watersmeet. Her eyes were keener than mine, and she spotted dippers and herons hidden away under the grass at the waters edge.

If you plant plenty of herbs, you will attract many moths and butterflies. I also have a soft spot for forsythia: I know it is common, but it cheers us all in spring, and if in January you break off a few bare branches they will open immediately indoors.

42   Grandchildren's trips

The first minibus trip was in 1983. It was always driven by Madge. This was the most important responsibility that she willingly undertook, and she was also the photographer. I did not take any children until they were four years old. They were expected to manage their own washing, dressing etc. I merely sat in the bus, played games with them and paid the bills.

We settled on buildings with an emphasis on why they were built. All reasons

COMBE 50

*This is to certify that the
bearer travelled from Combe
Halt on the occasion of the
station's 50th anniversary.*

COTSWOLD LINE PROMOTION GROUP

1985 saw the fiftieth anniversary of the opening of Combe Halt. As I travelled on the day it opened I was asked to take the same route on its important day. So I dressed as near as I could in my uniform, and the old basher was used again.

should begin with the letter 'P'. It was very simple.

We headed for Stratford upon Avon and found plays, preservation, poet (even a poacher), pedestrian bridge, pupils, the cathedral for prayer and praise and even the county hall built for public services. On we went to Ross on Wye; to the Prospect Gardens, a memorial to those who died of the plague. In Monmouth we saw almshouses built for the poor, a statue of Mr Charles Rolls, a pioneer of the car industry, standing on a plinth. In Chepstow we saw a portway and portcullis. Then into Wookey Hole (some pothole!) with pudding stone, on to Wells and the penniless porch, Bath with its pumproom, Pulteney bridge, the private houses of that palatial crescent. On the way home we called at the pigmy pinetum in Devizes and saw the polytunnel where conifers are propagated.

It was easy to find B and B and we were on tour for two nights. There were no behaviour problems because the children came from families living in different areas.

The following year we had one more added and we concentrated on rides and transport. We headed for Rhayader and Snowdon. We went to the summit, thence to Betws-y-coed and saw the swallow falls. We took a ride up the Great Orme, saw the smallest house and the village with the longest name. We went to the Centre for Alternative Technology, where the lift to enter is powered by a waterfall. We called at Llangollen on the way home and took a ride in a horse drawn barge on the canal.

The next year we had another one (now we were seven!). We headed for the Ironbridge area. We called first at Avoncroft – the open-air museum. We took the Severn Valley train from Bewdley to Bridgnorth. Blist's mill took a whole day but, staying at the same B and B we went to Coalport, saw the kilns, then on to R.A.F. Cosford. I remember this very well as the lady knew the boys were very keen on football, so she invited us in early to watch. Liverpool were playing in Belgium so we saw that awful tragedy. This was Oxford United's glorious year, when we won the milk cup and expected to be playing in Europe the following year. The awful behaviour of those Liverpool fans postponed that indefinitely. We called at the local butterfly farm on the way home.

The next year Madge, who lives in Harpenden, ordered the minibus and we drove there in our cars. First stop was Greenwich. We went over the Cutty Sark, then took a trip up the river to see the newly made flood barrier. Then to Canterbury – the cathedral and Roman walls. We noticed the hop fields and oast houses on the way to Dover. We saw the spot marked carefully where the first flight over the channel had rested, then spent a day around Dover Castle, saw the pharos and the dungeons. We even saw the barracks where Colin had once stayed.

The next year we decided to start from Godfrey's home in Manchester, to concentrate on the Yorkshire moors. We were there early in the morning and

Crossing Tarr Steps, Devon, with eight grandchildren.

early in the year so there were very few visitors. There was one other minibus carrying girl guides. We visited Hardraw Force, the tallest waterfall in England, the Aysgarth falls, then Brimham rocks. These sandstone rocks have been shaped over thousands of years by the wind. They are freaks of nature, superb for hide-and seek, but they are so striking and dramatic they deserve a trip for young or old. We had designs on a substantial walk this year and chose Malham Cove. It was nearly five miles but the children coped easily, not so the older ones. There were hundreds of steps to reach the Pennine limestone path at the top. Coming down amongst woods covered with wild garlic we approached Janet's Foss, another waterfall and pond evidently shared by many who enjoyed their birthday suits. It had a secluded atmosphere, surrounded by trees and spray and we were unaware of its existence.

We spent the next day in York, visiting the Minster, the Jorvik centre and the railway museum. I personally was so pleased to see 'The City of Truro' engine that had taken me to school about fifty years earlier. It was still being used and was in perfect condition. We called back at Ripon to see its hornblower, then to Ilkley Moor on the way back to Manchester.

The following year still with seven children we stopped for a meal at the cheese factory in Chewton Mendip. What a meal! Nine of us with plates full of cheese salad. How those boys laughed at the portions of cheese. We were heading for South Devon. Staying at Sidmouth we took a ride on a coastal tram, Cricket St Thomas offered an open air attraction including shire horses, crafts including wood turning and pottery, and a zoo. Plenty to see and do all day.

The Big Pit, north of Cardiff, with all nine grandchildren.

Then to Exmouth with boats of every type. This was extensive, the making and using of boats plus a museum of old ones. A sheep dairy farm amused us all, we tried out both the milk and cheese. We ambled home up the Cheddar Gorge.

The following year we took eight to Exmoor – the home of Lorna Doone. I knew this area as I had been twice with classes from school. We stopped at the Somerset levels, where we saw osiers growing, then being harvested. We even saw a basket being made from them. We encompassed most places mentioned in the Lorna Doone story – the robbers bridge, Oare church and Badgery water. We went horse riding, then on to Tarr Steps. We called at the honey farm on the way home.

My mother died in 1989 so my trips taking her out came to an abrupt end. And the trips with all the grandchildren only lasted one more year, as two of them were sixteen now and didn't really want a trip with gran. The next year was to be the last. The youngest, now four, was able to join, so for one year all nine of them came. The youngest was four and the eldest sixteen; seven boys and two girls. We went to St. Fagan's, the outdoor Welsh folk museum. This is a special place that appeals to all ages. I returned a year later to take Rose, Frank and George (Frank's brother) on a day trip.

Then we decided to try 'The Big Pit'. Now unused, it is a visitor centre, but quite an experience to go down. We decided to go to the hands-on exploratory centre. There was a resting area for adults. Madge and I made good use of it with a cup of coffee. The children were excited because all schools had written work to go into a second Domesday Book and now they each found their own

Les Robinson presenting me with a signed football on the occasion of our fiftieth wedding anniversary. Sadly Frank was unwell and unable to attend.

entry. There were many helpers there, and as we arrived so early in the day each child received individual attention.

I carried on a few more years, using my own car but just taking the younger ones. I enjoyed these trips. A holiday was impossible as Frank would not budge. He now walked very slowly but was very content to sit and read. In the bus we played games – pub tennis,[6] alphabet games, and sometimes we would sing.

Thank you to all Bed and Breakfast hosts who made our trips so memorable.

43   Change and decay

At the Manor Frank was beginning to feel the cold and for health reasons he would not be going again. Rose was pleased to occupy his seat.

My garden was covered with snowdrops; millions of them, and many neighbours and friends asked for some. I decided to sell them at the gate, charging fifty pence for each pot. That year alone I collected nearly £600 from snowdrops.

I decided to pay for a family outing. Brothers, sisters and grandchildren climbed aboard a coach to 'The Bloom's Nurseries' at Diss in Norfolk. Alan Bloom's sideline is steam. From miniatures to full-size steam trains, galloping

A trip for the elderly just reaching Brockhampton church, a few miles north of Ross-on-Wye. Although built about 1900, the design, the thatched roof and architecture outside was excelled only by the carving and embroidery inside. The churchyard was sprinkled with purple orchids.

horses and threshing tackle, there is interest for all. We did not quite fill the coach so I invited any elderly villagers to fill the empty seats. We all enjoyed it, especially me. I had taken so much from snowdrops I decided I would invite 'The Golden Leaves' (our pensioners' club) on another trip in the spring. I decided to keep on with these trips, the spring trip gives preference to 'The Golden Leaves' and the autumn trip gives first refusal to family and friends.

On February 6, 1995 I woke one morning to find Rose had not drawn her curtains. This was so unusual, I fetched her sister to delve into the cause. She was still in bed. I pulled back the cover to find she had passed away during the night.

A day out for the Golden Leaves.

This was a profound shock; she had walked to Blenheim on the previous day. I was approached to write an obituary in our village courier, as I knew her so well. We had started our lives together, went our different ways then finished them together.

I had already written this poem, it had just emerged from the sudden shock.

Just Rose

Rose took delight in a simple thing,
Faith, family, friends and a kettle to sing,
A football goal or a cricket wicket,
Pleasure in selling you a raffle ticket.
She visited many – not feeling so well,
Ran an errand or shopped or just sat a spell,
She sought out jobs, her time to fill,
Never mastering the art of sitting still.
She did nothing great; just helped every friend,
They knew on her they could always depend.
Rose never smoked, she was no alcoholic,
Hated scented soap, preferred old-fashioned carbolic.
We went on trips – just Rose and me,
But no five-star hotels, just one night B & B.
She was always eager to use her feet,
The Cotswold Way, Westonbirt or Watersmeet.
She hankered not for worldly wealth,
She even spurned the National Health.
She never really enjoyed the sun,
A crisp wintry day was much more fun.
In the eyes of the world, she was not that well blest
But she cultivated the seeds of happiness.
No foreign travel – just a walk in the wood,
No caviar – just plain apple pud,
No automobile – just a ride in a bus,
Death came, as she lived, without any fuss.

Rose had already extended the hand of friendship to Mary, a recently bereaved widow. She was shopping with us and sharing a cup of coffee. Rose's untimely death had thankfully thrown us together.

After Frank's spells of heart worries, in the spring of 1997 he suddenly improved. Colin and Linda and their two sons now took me to the Manor. I was using The Manor Club and they were using the exact seats that Frank and I used in the family area. My right hip was now giving me trouble. Would I have to undergo a hip replacement? The answer was 'Yes,' but there was a fourteen months wait.

On November 29th we all went as usual to see 'The Yellows play Port Vale'. Just before half time a message came over the speakers asking for me to go to the office. Rosie appeared and escorted me. I was handed the phone and was told by my brother in law that Frank had collapsed and died suddenly. He was eighty-seven years old.

Rosie understood and helped us in our emergency. Thank you very much; every club needs a 'Rosie' working with both the young and the bereaved.

I'd also like to say thank you to Pete who used to sit at the door of the Manor Club. One day as we drove to the Manor, our car was given a shove from behind. The car was damaged but still able to be driven. Colin's shoulder was injured. When we arrived at the Manor, Colin went to the medical unit. They whisked him off in the ambulance to the John Radcliffe.

Pete came to tell me and said, 'How will you get home?' 'I can drive, I'll go and pick him up at the end of the match,' I said.

'Where are the keys?' he questioned. 'I'll have to walk down and fetch them,' I said. At half time, Pete had already been to the hospital, found out what was happening and brought the keys back to me. 'Thank you Pete.'

Rosie and Pete are just two members of staff now at the Kassam, and they are typical of the family atmosphere that buzzes around; everyone seems to dovetail into a predetermined slot, no square pegs in round holes here. From the youngest member of a school group, to the school of excellence and its multitude of coaches, the youth teams and their coaches they are all on the same wavelength, all cogs in one wheel. I am just one of the oldest, least significant, but I still feel that I belong, like one blade of grass on that pitch.

Colin, now self-employed in gardening, is calling on me most days. My large area of trees, shrubs and flowers is a source of knowledge. My study of trees has not been in vain. What a blessing he has proved to be! He will replace a light bulb, open a difficult bottle or even clean out the guttering. Bridget calls, and after manoeuvring the carpet sweeper, she challenges me to a game of scrabble.

I actually waited ten months for my hip replacement. Unlike Frank, who had been a guinea pig some forty years earlier, mine was an instant success.

So many of us, like me, have to face the prospect of loneliness. This has to be faced realistically. So often I have heard, 'I just sit here looking at these four walls.' We are able to be positive. It is very easy for me as friends come to watch football or cricket on television. I've even had neighbours to watch my variety of birds. Three or four of us can gather for any reason, knitting squares, making a communal jigsaw, playing games like Monopoly or Bogle, or perhaps you have a valued videotape, or maybe you would prefer to read the Bible. We all have our preferences. I spend one afternoon a week playing scrabble and one playing whist.

We who have been chosen to live a long life, make sure companionship and mutual support gives a helping hand. Who is going to start the ball rolling? If

Above: Mary Skidmore, Peggy, Mary Seacole and yours truly playing Scrabble.
Below: Phyllis, David, Brian and Florrie playing whist at Long Hanborough.

you are the first, I guarantee a feeling of satisfaction, and anticipation of the next rendezvous.

The N.H.S. belongs to us all – it was our taxes that introduced it and have kept it going, though maybe it is struggling at the moment. Why is it struggling? Many say it is the fault of the government, many say there were not enough nurses trained in the eighties as they would be the elite nurses now. Some say too much is spent on research; our research is second to none. My father suffered with pernicious anaemia, he was given raw liver to eat, then he helped with research. Later, when it was confirmed that I had developed the same condition, I have one regular injection – no worry at all, thanks to Dad. Frank had three hip operations prior to two successful ones. When my hip faltered the first operation was a winner. I have a lot to thank the N.H.S. for.

If a bought a new car I wouldn't keep knocking dents into it. I think that is how we are treating our health service.

I sat by Frank's bed when he had his first operation. His leg was in traction. A lad of about nineteen was in the adjacent bed. He had just lost part of a leg in a motorbike accident. He was uncontrollable. I was very sorry for his mother. She had advised him against motorbikes, but he insisted he didn't care even if he killed himself. He had obviously not faced or even expected this situation. The bike was not paid for and his ability to earn money was gone.

Let's think who really is to blame? Is the N.H.S. too successful keeping too many of us alive for too long? Let's face it squarely; many of the hospital beds are filled with patients suffering from self-inflicted illnesses.

Are any of us – including myself – overweight? Do we eat too much, have too much fast food, or too little exercise? Do we smoke, drink too much alcohol or drive our car carelessly? Some are even guilty of unsafe sex!

We could all help to release those beds. Since the start of the N.H.S. the mileage that cars travel has probably multiplied by a hundred. We still grumble if the price of petrol goes up, but each injury on the road clogs up another bed. So in spite of all the overweights, the careless drivers, the fast food eaters, the idlers and the boozers, I salute the N.H.S. Let him without guilt throw the first stone.

I'd better jump on my exercise bike again.

44 *The Salt of the Earth*

This was my first book. It emerged from a project about Victorian times, which my mother, who had a superb memory, loved to reminisce about. She welcomed a listener but I welcomed the historic episodes that captured and brought back to life each necessary detail. Frank died in 1997 and my hip operation came in August 1998. But the book was written many years before these events.

Bridget, my youngest daughter, was now teaching at Ambrosden. History was repeating itself. She now took me out in the school holidays. Then she suggested that as I knew more about Victorian times than she did, she invited me to give talks to the pupils in Ambrosden.

'Like mother, like daughter.'

As Richard, her husband, had already put the book on computer disc she had read portions of it to her class. It was then that she gave me the ultimatum, 'If you don't publish the book – I shall.'

After making one or two enquiries, I went into the county museum in Woodstock. They put me in touch with Jon Carpenter and the ball started rolling. Thank you Jon.

The book was set in 1900 because my mother (Dora in the book) was six at the time as her family faced such a traumatic year. It was being published when the next millennium was looming but that was just coincidence. The book was conceived for educational purposes, and I hope in future will continue to be used for that purpose. It has sold well because the older generation love to read local history that, in some part, they can relate to.

My mother was scared of tuberculosis (T.B. to her) and rightly so. She did not worry about children's infectious ailments. She blamed so many deaths from these complaints both on bad nursing and bad housing. Houses were very small and families very large. Can we imagine the difficulties they faced? Several houses in Combe now were actually three houses when I first remember them.

Since my schooldays, most infectious diseases have been eradicated including diphtheria and scarlet fever. The anti-flu jab is very successful. Glaucoma can now be arrested, cataracts terminated, pneumonia is no longer dreaded.

If you yearn for the good old days, do you visualise old ladies, nearly blind, sitting in wicker chairs, wetting themselves because they could not move? I remember a sixty-year-old man who still stumbled around although his back was at a ninety-degree angle. He didn't go to bed because he couldn't climb the twisted steps.

So much has been conquered in one lifetime. It can only happen again if we take charge of our own destiny.

45   Into the Kassam Stadium

The eighties were the heyday of Oxford United. Committed season ticket holders now, Frank and I did not miss a match. We often travelled to away matches. It was a hobby that we both enjoyed. We did vary our seating positions but eventually we found the back row in the family enclosure to our liking. We each had our idols changing with the years. I still think Maurice Kyle and Colin Clarke took a lot of beating in defence.

The award-winning side of 1986 was the best all-round team we ever produced. Frank insisted that Kevin Brock was the most influential (let's forget that one back-pass). I have always thought the ability to know where your colleagues are is the mark of the craftsman.

What is the use of manoeuvring the ball pass several players only to be floored at the last hurdle? I think the last accurate pass to a player in a scoring

The first match at the Kassam stadium against Crystal Palace finished in favour of Oxford after a penalty shoot-out.

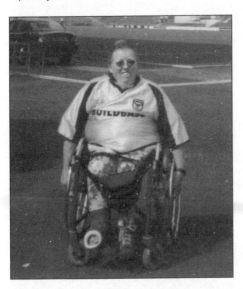

Maureen spent her schooldays at the Penhurst school for the disabled in Chipping Norton, from where she was often brought to the Manor. Now, having settled in North London, she attends regularly. She drives herself the sixty miles to the stadium and gets into her wheelchair unaided, and she often attends away matches as well. Recently she caught the supporters' coach to Darlington, a round trip of about 700 miles. What a dedicated fan! And listening to that game on the radio, I could easily single out her voice...

position should somehow be better rewarded.

I well remember Brian Clough talking about his Nottingham Forest cup winning team. He was a passionate and very positive manager. Calculating his season's goals, 65% were scored by speed alone, 30% came from set pieces, corners, free kicks and penalties and only 5% came from normal play. A team should take the field with the determination to score. Experience does not score goals – in defence it can save many but initiative and speed are the strikers' attributes.

My memory tells me we have beaten every team in the league except Liverpool. Who remembers the first day that Alec Ferguson took over Manchester

The re-union of the Milk Cup produced this cheque for charity.

United? Gary Briggs brought the ball down the field, half the strikers went to the left and half to the right, and the defenders went with them. Just like the waters of the Red Sea, they parted and, like the Israelites, Gary freewheeled down the centre and scored. Among memorable goals was David Langan's against Arsenal,

The palatial Kassam stadium showing the multi-purpose conference centre.

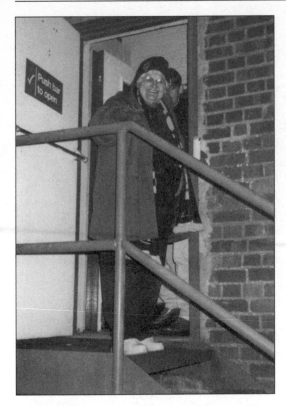

After the firework display in 2000 I descend the Manor steps for the last time.

Jeoy Beachamp's against Blackpool – or who would ever forget Peter Rhoades-Brown's (now called Rosie) against his old club, Chelsea? Who remembers Chrissie Allen accelerating down the wing and scoring in the dying seconds to level the score five each. Then Dean Saunders, with the help of John Dreyer, scoring in extra time at Ipswich.

I think the biggest disappointment was against Chelsea when Dean Windass had given us the lead only to be thwarted by a penalty handed out so freely.

The goals at Wembley are still very clear in my mind and the Milk Cup still stands proudly in the Kassam Stadium.

During these years, as one large family, Oxford were fighting together for survival and a new ground. We wore yellow ribbons at one spell, we gathered at Garsington for a public enquiry, sites were investigated everywhere. How many home produced players had to be sold to keep us afloat! Until recently I had boasted that every premiership club had benefited from Oxford except Manchester United but they did use Ron Atkinson as manager. Then they scrounged Steve McClaren from us via Derby.

Walking in my garden one day I saw a father pushing a buggy. Having seen a sticker in my car he introduced himself to me. It was Les Robinson. We became friends, and he would often bring his son Liam to play football on our lawn. At the age of two Liam knew his right and left foot. He also knew he had to use both of them.

Thank you Les (I never call him Robbo) for all that good defending, on the halfway line when Oxford attacked, at the goalpost when Oxford defended. We remember those runs down to that sloping corner to London Road end. More than ten of his best years were given to Oxford. Is it too late to reward him?

Welcome to Firoz Kassam. Many doubted his ability to change things around. 'Why doesn't he put his hand in his pocket?' many fans said. I always

The School of Excellence runs eight schoolboy teams, from the under-9s to the under-17s. It also monitors their educational progress. It is the source of many past, present and future players.

thought he had his priorities right, I recognised immediately a shrewd financier who would secure the roots of the club. Many said, 'He is only here for what he can get.' What a statement! What can anyone get from a nearly bankrupt club with a half-built stadium and court battles looming? Oxford's only asset was the Manor Ground. If, in the future, he does make money from Oxford, well done! Because this is mutual, if he does well, Oxford will be doing well. I hope my last few years will see Oxford climbing again.

At least, I'm not like Moses, he did not enter 'The Promised Land'.

Thank you to all who helped in any way to the efforts of F.O.U.L. (Fighting for Oxford United's Life).

When I first saw the new stadium, I was overwhelmed: emotion swelled inside me. Crowds were already queuing. We found a very nice young man named Chris Ellis who gave us a complete tour. It compares with the best in the country. Mr Kassam is preparing a home for all of us impatient yet expectant fans. He is taking pride in all that he does. Some home! When he spends he buys the best. What a stadium! What a pitch! Thank you! Thank you! He cannot possibly spend all this money to allow us to wallow in the third division.

To those whingeing fans; think of a ladder when you erect it, it must be secured. We've been up that ladder, either one or two rungs, once to the top but it has always collapsed on us. This time it is well anchored.

To all those singers in the stadium, we like you, but please try new songs that will make us smile. Should the ref give us a penalty, try singing 'Who do we like? We like you ref.' Use the tune of Westminster chimes. You never know, he might be amused. I doubt if any fans of any club ever liked the ref before, he just might give us another penalty.

46   Pleasures of life

I'm omitting the pleasures of babies, a process that is natural to all females although very rewarding.

In teaching I've experienced the most pleasure in teaching children to read. The glow on their faces, the light in their eyes and the addiction that comes with knowledge confirms that you are winning. I've always worked on the principle that if you can teach a child the desire to read, you have overcome the worst obstacle. I loved doing it and I always found it easy.

I recall a lad at the age of five telling me that his Dad couldn't read so he had decided that he wouldn't read. When I asked him what he hoped to do as an adult, he said, 'Be a milkman, so I won't need to read.'

When we settled to start reading, I put him at a desk alone. I had written the words 'One pint please' on a card. 'There you are,' I said, 'You must copy that, because you will have to read the notes put out by customers.'

He sat methodically writing and re-writing the words. I praised him and wrote another card for the next day. This continued for about ten days, then quite suddenly he came to me during the lesson. In the most disbelieving tone he said, 'I'm learning to read, aren't I?'

He could not comprehend that reading was not difficult.

The next incident was a bright six-year-old who was confident and understood her reading. At this stage I told children to read a whole sentence, missing out the difficult word, and by sounding the first few letters you can usually guess the word that fits.

She came to the sentence: 'Penny saw something str... in her garden.' Doing exactly as I had said she read it several times, her face lit up, I knew she had guessed it. 'Penny saw something strordinary in her garden.' I did not intervene, I thought reading with sense was more important than one word. I just smiled, and I knew her reading was conquered.

While at Cogges school I remember an assembly one morning when the head mistress talked about prayer. The whole group discussed sensible topics that would influence the whole world. They were asked to write their own prayer asking for what they thought was most desirable. One eight-year-old in my class wrote, 'Please God send good weather for the fishermen so they can catch lots of fish. Please send sun and rain for the farmers then they can grow lots of potatoes. Then everyone can have plenty of fish and chips.' Did he get his priorities right?

Adults don't always believe me, but do they hope to prove me wrong?

There is Ruby, who bought my book *Born in a Stable*. She clearly thought it was too far fetched to believe, till older people in Freeland verified it. She came back to me saying, 'It's absolutely true,' as if I didn't know.

And the pleasure of the birds that have come to my garden. On November

My family today. Back row: Bridget, Godfrey, Colin, Madge. Front row: their spouses Pat, Richard, Linda, Michael.

9th 1994 I saw a ring ouzel feeding on my berries. I rang John Brucker, the ornithologist, who for years had been my headmaster. 'No,' he said, 'They have all emigrated by now, and they don't come near habitation.' As I persisted he came to see it, just to enlighten me on the bird. His reaction when he saw it was incredible. He had always been Mr Brucker to me, we had only met in class-rooms with our minds devoted to education. Here he was in my multi-purpose room telling me what I already knew, it was a ring ouzel. He was behaving like a youngster with a new toy. He was human after all. The ring ouzel did stay for ten days and many came to view it.

Sorry John – notice it's his Christian name now – thank you very much for the framed picture.

Last of all, quite recently Brian Hodgson, another retired schoolmaster, asked to watch a football match on my television. He is a lifelong supporter of Charlton – living many miles away he still has a season ticket. This particular day Charlton were playing at Highbury. He had never been to Highbury, so, all arranged, he came to view.

Brian sat well back in his chair, knowing that his team had very little chance, so when Arsenal scored, well, it was expected. Then Charlton scored one and another before half-time. Brian edged a little closer to the front of his chair. 'I can't believe this,' he said, clapping his hands. We both expected the worst in the second half but Charlton had other ideas. They overran Arsenal, scoring another. Brian's feet were twitching, he edged nearer the television. I was enjoying the match, but watching Brian was much more entertaining. Then

Charlton scored again, Brian jumped up and danced around in typical Martin O'Neill style: he didn't need a chair now. What a commotion for a few goals! Charlton won that match 4-2. I'll forgive him because I remember Dave Langan's goal that gave us a win over Arsenal.

Lastly, I have always enjoyed trips around Britain, first the caravan trips with my own children, then the minibus trips with the grandchildren, and now just day trips with those who, like me, tend to reminisce. That multi-purpose room now acts as a bird hide, all are welcome.

47   Conclusion

Combe still presides over its little hill around the village green. No animals cross the green any more, but the village fair still arrives on the tenth of August, as does the maypole dancing and the bonfire in their season.

Only the one inn now, The Cock Inn, welcomes all customers including many who are walking the Oxfordshire Way. The cricket field still attracts the teams but alas the standard of cricket reaches those dizzy heights no more. The school is still in use, now classified as a beacon school. Twenty-five pupils on the 1929 photograph but it now boasts a register of 108. There is now both a toddler and a pre-school group.

The women's institute is still active and even its market stall still opens its doors each Friday in Woodstock. We still have a part-time post office but only one small shop. We have a monthly newsletter which was instigated by Christine and Rob Smith in 1985. The *Combe Courier* has proved very useful.

The Reading Room – or Tavern – is still in constant use by the local council and village organisations. The elderly use it on Tuesdays. One week each month for The Golden Leaves, the other Tuesdays for games, cards and scrabble.

The railway halt is still in use, but the siding to the sawmill has long since gone. All timber is now transported by road. This railway line is the main Paddington to Worcester line – only a single track now. Scrub has grown up on the embankments where the ganger and his navvies once worked daily. I can even see an oak tree about twenty feet high. Only the remains of the original fencing survives that was erected some 100 years ago. Isambard Kingdom Brunel would be ashamed.

The river Evenlode still meanders and ambles its way around the meadows, very similar to the old men who had over celebrated that I remember from my youth. Hundreds of gallons of water from a superb spring is transported around the country in huge unwelcome lorries.

Gamekeepers are fast disappearing, all those so-called pests of the animal and bird world are now allowed to breed without human interference.

The bird population has changed dramatically; the last twenty years has witnessed the decline of the grey partridge and the green plover. They do not like the planting of winter corn. We always saw the occasional green woodpecker but greater spotted and even lesser spotted have overtaken their numbers. Like the tits they have benefited from our generosity. The local bog near the Evenlode has been drained so sadly we see no more snipe or curlew.

Although most of us do not think highly of the yellow fields of rape, they do encourage more insects, which in turn attract the hobby. It can be seen in the summer dipping over the crops. Sadly rape also multiplies the population of flea beetles – really enormous specimens that invade the gardens in spring.

During the long summer days, when in the fields, my sister and I would make our own 'bee gardens'. We each measured a square yard and then picked the best wild flowers we could find. We pushed them into the ground, then waited for the bees. We usually attracted twenty or thirty, but we learnt which flowers were most successful. Scabious and knapweed were good but wild thyme always proved the best.

At the time of my birth the population of Combe was 429. Many inhabitants married and carried on living in the village. During this period many small cottages were modernised and two or even three were converted to single dwellings. More than 200 new homes have been built and the population now exceeds 800. Gas has never been brought to the village. And being positioned on the top of the hill means that never ever will we be flooded.

Unless something unforeseen occurs, both my maiden and married names will disappear from Combe. This is partly due to the fact that the male side of the families have produced more females, but a combination of easier transport and much improved education has helped to scatter the families far and wide.

Glossary

1   The mill. This is the Blenheim saw mill. At that time timber was transported by rail so it had its own private side line.

2   M and B tablets. I think these were the forerunner of antibiotics.

3   Thrums were ends of wool used for carpet making.

4   Baritone is used either as a bass instrument for tenor horns or as a lighter type of euphonium. It is pitched in B flat.

5   The rounders. this patch of grass was created by horses as the hill was too steep for them to descend with a wagon load of coal. It was an ideal place for picnics, many types of orchid, *campanula glomerata* and quaker grass grew there. Alas, now it is covered by scrub.

6   Pub tennis, a game we played on the minibus. The left side of the bus was playing against the right. Each pub that appeared added one point.

7   Square cake. When Bridget was nearly three she came in from the garden asking for something to eat. Unable to remember the name she described it as 'square cake'. It was really bread pudding which I always made in a square tin. As the family still ask for it today, I give you my recipe:

½ loaf of bread or equivalent in crusts (I use white)

250 grams of large raisins

2 eggs

1 teaspoon allspice

½ teaspoon cinnamon

1 teacup of sugar (I use soft brown)

In those bygone days I used raisins with stones but you can still purchase large juicy ones at a health food store. They are expensive but nothing else is as good.

Soak the bread in water and pour off the surplus, do not squeeze. Add all the other ingredients, then plunge in your hands and mix. Place in a greased container.

Place one or two very small knobs of fat on top.

The art of cooking is to do it very slowly. Place in a cold oven, turn the heat to 200°, when it has reached that point turn off the heat, don't open the oven door. Leave it in the oven for at least another hour. It is best eaten immediately but is still very nice cold.

8   Clamp – a long mound of potatoes placed on straw and covered with it, then enveloped with soil to keep out the frost in the winter.

9   Shock – in some counties called a stook. It was six or eight sheaves of corn propped together with the ears uppermost. They were left two or three

weeks or until dry. This prevented the rick heating and causing mould to the corn.

10   Thermogene. A very thick, pink woven material, it was soft, similar to cotton wool and bought by the yard. It was heavily disinfected with iodine – everyone knew when I was wearing it. It was supposed to generate heat and keep germs away; it felt like a poultice.

11   Squibs were tubes – similar to toothpaste tubes – made of lead. They were filled with water and used profusely at fairs.

12   Corn rick. This was the stack of sheaves that was built professionally, then thatched to keep out rain.

13   Broody hen. When a hen has laid her first batch of eggs in the spring, nature encourages her to sit on a clutch of eggs to hatch them. Nowadays an incubator is used, but hens kept solely to lay eggs are given artificial lights so they are expected to lay one egg every day of their life. The eggs would be of little use for producing the next generation because the hens never see a cockerel.

14   Knottoaks. The name of a local wood with a small keeper's bungalow near it. There was usually a partridge keeper living there.

15   Peg Rug. This is a homemade rug with a base of hessian, usually a potato sack. Snippets of tweed were freely available after a small boy's short trousers were produced from an old garment brought home from service. The small pieces were cut about an inch wide and three inches long, and according to colour were pegged into the hessian, sometimes quite artistically. The finished article was very warm and heavy, but very, very dusty.

16   Dickey seat. This was originally the servant's seat at the back of a horse-drawn carriage but some early cars had seats at the back that could be closed when not in use. In use they were always open to the elements.